HOCKEY'S HOTTEST DEFENSEMEN

Their Stories On and Off the Ice

HOCKEY'S HOTTEST DEFENSEMEN

Their Stories On and Off the Ice

J. Alexander Poulton

OVER TIME BOOKS

First printed in 2007 10 9 8 7 6 5 4 3 2 1
Printed in Canada

The Publisher: OverTime Books is an imprint of Éditions de la Montagne Verte

Library and Archives Canada Cataloguing in Publication

Poulton, J. Alexander (Jay Alexander), 1977–
Hockey's hottest defensemen / J. Alexander Poulton.

Includes bibliographical references.
ISBN-13: 978-1-897277-27-0
ISBN-10: 1-897277-27-X

1. Hockey players—Biography. 2. National Hockey League—Biography. 3. Hockey—Defense. I. Title.

GV848.5.A1P695 2007 796.962092'2 C2007-904331-3

Project Director: J. Alexander Poulton
Proofreader: Tara Woloschuk
Production: Alexander Luthor
Cover Image: Photograph by Winslow Townson/CP

PC: P5

Contents

Introduction

It is the position in hockey that has some of the highest pressure to perform and the least amount of glory for a job well done. A team may have a forward line of some of the greatest scorers in the game, but without solid defenders backing them up, the team remains incomplete. All the great teams in hockey history have had some of the best defenders ever to step on a blue line: the early incarnation of the Ottawa Senators had defensive stalwarts Eddie Gerard and Harvey Pulford to guide them through their most dominant years; the Boston Bruins of the late 1920s and 1930s were feared simply because of one man, Eddie Shore; the Montréal Canadiens' domination of the 1950s was quarterbacked by arguably the greatest defenseman ever, Doug Harvey; the Toronto Maple Leafs of the 1960s had the always-reliable Tim Horton; and the resurgent Canadiens of the 1970s could rely on the greatest team of defensemen—Larry Robinson, Guy Lapointe and Serge Savard. As you continue down the list of Stanley Cup champions, it is evident that a team must have a group of solid blueliners to get anywhere close to raising the Stanley Cup.

The Edmonton Oilers' run in the 2006 Stanley Cup playoffs is the perfect example of the need for a solid defensive line if a team is to have any success in the post-season. With Chris Pronger on the team, the Oilers were able to secure themselves a playoff spot. No one expected that the team would make it far into the playoffs, but with each game the Oilers played, it was apparent that they could successfully take on the best teams in the league. The Oilers' first challenge was the high-powered Detroit Red Wings, and they met it with a solid defense led by Pronger and his defensive partner, captain Jason Smith, defeating the Wings in six games. As the quarterback for the Oilers' offensive rushes, Chris Pronger helped the Oilers pass the San Jose Sharks and the Anaheim Ducks and reach a seventh game in the Stanley Cup finals against the Carolina Hurricanes. Just one season later, Pronger left the Oilers to join the Anaheim Ducks, and while the Oilers had to watch the playoffs from the comfort of their homes, Pronger was working his way through each round on the way to his first-ever Stanley Cup.

For most of the 1990s, NHL teams looked to stock their blue lines with large defensemen who were more able to push a player off a puck than move with the flow of the game and contribute to the offense. In the 1990s, the focus in the National Hockey League on the ice was on defense: slow down the offensive players by clogging the neutral zone with large, immovable defensemen. Players like Derian Hatcher, Rob Blake and Zdeno Chara, all of whom are over six feet tall, were what most teams in the league looked for. But when the league altered its rules in 2004 to allow a more offensive style of play, many of these defensemen found that their once-sought-after skills were now holding them back.

In the first few weeks after hockey returned following the 2004–05 lockout, it became apparent that the era of the big defenseman was in jeopardy. The big blueliners would have to adapt to the new game or risk losing their jobs. Defensemen such as the Toronto Maple Leafs' Hal Gill and the Montréal Canadiens' Sheldon Souray looked like they had cement in their skates as the speedier players had their way with them on several occasions, stick handling the puck through them for a few highlight reel goals. Some of the bigger guys have survived and even thrived in the new-rules NHL, but teams are moving toward smaller, more mobile defensemen for the future of the league.

The Buffalo Sabres and the Philadelphia Flyers are two examples on opposite ends of the win column that illustrate the new reality for NHL defensemen. The Buffalo Sabres have built one of the most successful teams in the NHL with a highly skilled and highly mobile defense. Players such as Brian Campbell and Jaroslav Spacek, both under six feet tall and weighing less than 200 pounds, are able to add an offensive side to their game, making the Buffalo attack one of the most effective in the league. The Philadelphia Flyers decided to go big on defense, hoping that two large blueliners would be able to stop three speedy forwards. However, with players such as Derian Hatcher, at six feet, five inches tall and 237 pounds dry, and Braydon Coburn, at six feet, five inches tall and 225 pounds dry, the Flyers' defense was one of the worst in the league during the entire 2006–07 season.

Four years ago, the list of defensemen considered the hottest in the league would have looked entirely different from today; Rob Blake and Derian Hatcher would have made that list easily. Although there is still space in the NHL for big defensemen, the league now belongs to younger, more mobile players such as the Calgary Flames'

Dion Phaneuf and the Montréal Canadiens' Andrei Markov. In the following pages, I have listed some of the best defensemen in the NHL today, from 45-year-old defensive veteran Chris Chelios to new-kid-on-the-block Ryan Whitney. There are players that some people will feel should have made the list, but know that I chose these players carefully, not just for their names or how many goals they scored, but for what they contributed to their team both on and off the ice. Although a forward's job is simply to move the puck down the ice and stick it in the net (a little oversimplified, but it illustrates the point), a defenseman has to look at all aspects of the game and, with just his line mate, protect his end of the ice. A good defenseman can contribute to his team in a way no other player on the ice can.

Chapter One

Dion Phaneuf
The Monster

When he retired from his blueline position with the New Jersey Devils in September 2005, players in the league breathed a collective sigh of relief. No longer would they have to worry that a brick wall by the name of Scott Stevens was waiting to pounce on them as soon as their skates crossed into his territory. Stevens' career highlight reels are filled with countless examples of players crossing into the New Jersey defensive zone with their heads down, more focused on watching their pretty pass rather than looking out for the freight train barreling down on them from their blind side. Just ask Eric Lindros and Paul Kariya what it felt like to be on the other end of a Scott Stevens check—if they remember.

But as players started to relax and prepare for the start of the 2005–06 season after the previous season's lockout, they began to hear whispers of a young up-and-comer who was looking to take up the spot left vacant by Stevens. Like Stevens, a man he has expressed admiration for, this young upstart could score, had a blistering slap shot and could deliver a body check that would send even the biggest players flying to the ice. No one would ever wish to be on the receiving end of one of his hits.

Dion Phaneuf began playing hockey at an early age in his hometown of Edmonton, Alberta, and because of his size, he was naturally suited for a spot on the blue line. His coaches knew that one day he would make a fierce competitor because of his dedication to the game and his above-average slap shot. His coaches were right: soon, Dion Phaneuf was ripping up the Western Hockey League with the Red Deer Rebels.

At six feet, three inches tall and weighing 200 pounds, Phaneuf was a physical force on the team but struggled during 2001-02, his first year in the bigger and faster WHL. He had the tendency to over-skate the puck, and when an opponent came in on the attack, he would play the puck instead of the man, leading to some occasional odd-man rushes. He scored only 5 goals and 12 assists. Some other defensemen might consider that a decent showing for their first year, but Phaneuf was the consummate professional and worked hard during the off-season to get up to the level he knew he could attain.

With a renewed sense of purpose, Phaneuf returned to the Red Deer Rebels and scored 16 goals and 14 assists. But it wasn't just his offensive output that was starting to get the attention of the other teams in the league. The old Phaneuf would most of the time try to pole the puck away from an attacking forward crossing into the Rebels defensive zone, but now Phaneuf began to employ the Scott Stevens method of defending: he made every forward in the league aware of his presence on the ice. In the next two seasons, Phaneuf became one of the best defensemen in the WHL and one of the top prospects for the 2003 NHL entry draft.

The 2003 draft year was rife with talent, and it was anyone's guess as to which players would be the most sought after. The Pittsburgh Penguins had the first selection and chose goaltender Marc-André Fleury, and, as the selections went by, those who had seen Phaneuf play were surprised that no team had yet chosen him. Second selection went to the Carolina Hurricanes, who chose Eric Staal, and third choice went to the Florida Panthers, who selected Nathan Horton. Surely Phaneuf would go with the fourth and fifth selections, which belonged to the Columbus

Blue Jackets and the Buffalo Sabres, but still he sat nervously in the stands waiting for his name to be called. Eight teams selected other players before the Calgary Flames finally got their chance, and, to their surprise, Phaneuf was still available. Having scouted Phaneuf, the Flames knew how lucky they were to still have the option of selecting the bruiser of a defenseman. Going ninth overall did not matter to Phaneuf; all he cared about was that he had a path to the National Hockey League.

The Flames had the option of bringing Phaneuf, just 19 years old, up to the pros right away, but they felt he still needed some time in the WHL to work on the finer points of his game—and work he did. In 2004, he was awarded the WHL's Bill Hunter Memorial Trophy for the top defenseman after a stellar season, scoring 19 goals and 24 assists. Phaneuf turned heads at the 2004 World Junior Championship, playing for Team Canada and helping them get to the final game against the American team. It was the Americans, however, who got to throw their gloves and sticks in the air at the end of the game, beating out the Canadians for the gold.

Phaneuf would have been called up to the Calgary Flames for the start of the 2004–05 season, but the players and NHL management could not agree on a collective bargaining contract, and the season was locked out. Phaneuf returned for another season in the WHL with the Red Deer Rebels, and in just 55 games, he managed to improve upon his previous year's totals, this time with 24 goals and 32 assists, for 56 points. The Calgary Flames could call up Phaneuf for the 2005–06 season with full confidence that he was ready for the big league.

But Phaneuf had one last thing to accomplish before moving up to the NHL and joining the Flames for training camp. In the middle of his final season with the Red Deer Rebels, Phaneuf was named to the Canadian men's junior team for the 2005 World Junior Championship, held in Grand Forks, North Dakota. Phaneuf, along with teammates Sidney Crosby and Patrice Bergeron, helped Canada walk away with the gold for the first time in eight years, going down as possibly the best collection of juniors ever to put on the Canadian jersey. Phaneuf finished the tournament with 1 goal and 5 assists and took home the award for the top defenseman. Brimming with confidence, he was ready to take on the NHL.

Phaneuf made his first appearance on the Flames' opening night against the Minnesota Wild on October 5, 2005. Just a few days later, he recorded his first goal and first assist in the NHL on October 10 against the Colorado Avalanche. Within the first few games of his arrival, it was clear that a new force had entered the NHL. Phaneuf dominated physically from the outset of the season, delivering hits and quarterbacking plays like a seasoned veteran. His commitment to the team and making his presence known on the ice earned him the NHL's Rookie of the Month Award for November, which is not a bad accomplishment considering Sidney Crosby and Alexander Ovechkin were lighting up the league with their flashy goal scoring. Seeing how Phaneuf played with such passion and power, the Flames must have regretted not having him in the lineup for their run to the Stanley Cup finals in 2004 because with him on the team, they were far better off.

Game after game, Phaneuf delivered the big hits, defended his end of the ice like a veteran and used his howitzer of a slap shot to score an incredible 20 goals and 29 assists, making him a prime candidate for Rookie of the Year considerations. His 20 goals put him in a class with players such as Brian Leetch and Barry Beck as the only defensemen to score 20 or more goals in their rookie seasons. But with 52 goals and 54 assists, Alexander Ovechkin was given the Calder Trophy as Rookie of the Year.

During his second season alone, Phaneuf established himself as one of the premier defensemen in the league, and he received a nomination to the 2007 All-Star game to prove it. At the end of the 2006–07 season, Phaneuf had recorded another fine year, with 17 goals, 33 assists and a plus/minus rating of +10. There is no doubt that with his talent, drive and ability to put the fear of God into some players, Phaneuf will one day be a Norris Trophy winner and, if the stars align, a Stanley Cup champion.

Season	Team	GP	Goals	Assists	Points	+/-	Penalties
2005–06	Calgary	82	20	29	49	5	93
2006–07	Calgary	79	17	33	50	10	98

Chapter Two

Scott Niedermayer

The Best All-Round Defenseman

Scott Niedermayer was born in Edmonton, Alberta, on August 31, 1973, but grew up in Cranbrook, British Columbia. Like so many Canadian kids, Niedermayer immediately took to playing hockey in the wintertime. And like so many Canadian parents, the Niedermayers would wake up very early every weekend to take their kids to hockey practice, never once thinking that one day their children would be among the top players in the NHL. But when you see the way Scott Niedermayer skates today, it should come as no surprise that he was born to be a hockey player.

Niedermayer cut his proverbial teeth in the Canadian youth hockey system and was quickly noted as one of the standout players. While other kids his age were skating well enough to compete, Niedermayer could skate circles around most of them. His natural ability on skates and his graceful puck movement got him noticed by the Western Hockey League's Kamloops Blazers, who signed him without hesitation. In Kamloops, Niedermayer blossomed into the player he is today, suppressing his desire to use his speed and join the rush on every occasion and instead playing the position smart by sitting back most of the time and opting to pinch in only when the play dictated.

Growing up, Niedermayer never had one particular player he admired, preferring to select traits from a bunch of players and try to incorporate them into his game. "Perhaps Mario Lemieux and Paul Coffey as well. Those guys were probably my favorite players growing up," said Niedermayer in an interview, looking back on his early days. "I enjoy playing defense. I don't see myself ever changing positions." Niedermayer always knew he had the offensive talent to play as a forward, but it was the challenge of the defensive position that kept him on the blue line.

Niedermayer helped make the Kamloops Blazers the best team in the WHL and contributed on their path to the Memorial Cup in 1990 and 1992. With a player like Niedermayer, who could score like the top forward on the team and skate back to defend like an NHL veteran, it was easy to see how the Blazers could walk away with two Memorial Cups in the span of three seasons. During his first year with the Blazers, Niedermayer scored an incredible 14 goals and 55 assists in just 64 games. One season later, he greatly improved on his previous totals by scoring 26 goals and 54 assists in only 57 games.

With stats like that, it wasn't long before the stands at the Blazers games were full of eager scouts waiting to talk to the rushing defenseman, who had some of them making comparisons to the greatest rushing defenseman of all time, Bobby Orr. When it came time for Niedermayer to put on his suit and go down to the 1991 NHL entry draft, most of the attention was being paid to the big phenomenon from the Oshawa Generals, Eric Lindros. The Québec Nordiques had the first selection and had made it clear that they were going to select Lindros, but when he refused to sign on with the club, the media got lost in the frenzy of words that ensued from both the Lindros camp and the Nordiques camp. When Niedermayer was selected third overall by the New Jersey Devils, barely anyone noticed, but he went on to take home the Canadian Hockey League's Player of the Year Award in 1991 and a Memorial Cup in 1992, along with the Stafford Smythe Memorial Trophy as the Most Valuable Player in the Memorial Cup tournament.

Niedermayer joined the Devils for the 1992–93 season as a fresh-faced 19-year-old rookie. He had played just four games for the Devils in the 1991–92 season, but he got the green light to join the regular team the next season after a solid training camp, during which he impressed the coaching staff with his level of maturity as a rookie defenseman. Amazingly, Niedermayer played in all 80 games that season and was one of the outstanding rookies in the league; unfortunately, Teemu Selanne's 76 goals earned him the Calder Trophy as Rookie of the Year. Despite the trophy snub, Niedermayer's statistics were up there with the best defensemen in the league: he finished his rookie season with 11 goals, 29 assists and a plus/minus rating of +8, reassuring to the Devils coaching staff that the rookie was going to be a part of their organization's push for a Stanley Cup for years to come.

Niedermayer got to extend his year with his first taste of the post-season in the first round of the playoffs against the defending champions, the Pittsburgh Penguins. But his dream of battling it out in the playoffs all the way to the Stanley Cup would end all too quickly. The Penguins handed the young Devils a harsh lesson by eliminating them in five games, but it was a lesson the Devils would learn from, returning to the playoffs over the next few years a much better team for having taken that crushing defeat at the hands of Mario Lemieux and Jaromir Jagr.

During the off-season, the Devils changed head coaches and, in the process, changed the fortunes of the team for the next couple of years. When Jacques Lemaire played in the NHL for the Montréal Canadiens, he was always known as a defensive player even though he was on a forward line. He was a big reason the Montréal Canadiens of the late 1970s achieved the great successes they did. Now, as a coach, Lemaire wanted to impart some of his defensive wisdom on the New Jersey Devils players by imposing a highly defensive strategy that quickly earned a fitting moniker: the trap. The trap is a system employed by all the players on the ice that is intended to stop the forward progression of the opponents through the neutral zone. This system proved very effective for the Devils, and although it stifled Niedermayer's offensive talents, his defensive side shone brightly. For the 1993–94 season, his plus/minus rating went from +8 the previous season to an incredible +34.

Under the new system, the Devils became one of the better teams in the league and, for the first time in their franchise's history, a serious contender for the Stanley Cup. They finished the season in second place overall behind the New York

Rangers and faced off against the Buffalo Sabres in the first round of the playoffs. Niedermayer's offensive skills were put aside in favor of pure defense. It was a very defense-oriented series that went all the way to game seven, and luckily, the Devils came out on top with a narrow 2–1 victory in the final game. The Devils then handed the Boston Bruins their golf passes with a six-game series victory to move on to the conference finals against the New York Rangers. This series had all the makings of a classic battle, and the two top teams in the Eastern Conference did not disappoint. After the first four games, New Jersey took the lead in the series by winning the fifth game 4–1. But Rangers captain Mark Messier led his team through a nail-biting comeback to win the series in the seventh game in double overtime. Niedermayer and the Devils would have to wait for another year to attempt a run at the Cup.

They had to wait until January 1995 for the season to get underway because of complications between NHL management and the NHL Players' Association, but when the season started, Niedermayer had another stellar defensive year, helping the Devils into a good position at the start of the 1995 post-season. After dispensing with the Boston Bruins in the first round of the playoffs, the Devils finally felt like they had the elements needed to make it far; they just had to stay healthy and keep Martin Brodeur happy. Pittsburgh proved to be another easy series for the Devils, who won it in five games. The Philadelphia Flyers had an equally difficult time with the Devils' defensive system in the conference finals and succumbed to the pressure in six games, putting the Devils in the Stanley Cup finals for the first time in their history.

The Detroit Red Wings were quickly becoming one of the hardest teams in the league to beat and were not about to let the Devils walk away with the Cup. The Red Wings were coached by the legendary Scotty Bowman, who had seen, developed and beaten all kinds of hockey systems before and was not fazed by the Devils' defensive trap system. Despite his confidence in his players, Bowman did not give enough credit to the defensive core of the Devils. Niedermayer and fellow blueliners Scott Stevens and Tommy Albelin practiced the trap system to perfection, keeping the Red Wings' scoring chances to a minimum while Martin Brodeur did the rest. The Red Wings were swept away in four games, and Niedermayer had his first Stanley Cup just three years into his career.

Things continued in an upward trend for Niedermayer as he continued to improve his play, and, in the process, he earned the respect of players throughout the league. In 1997 and 1998, he was elected to the NHL All-Star game and was a constant threat during the skills competition as one of the fastest skaters in the league. The Devils continued their regular-season successes, but the playoffs had a way of disappointing them each year with early first- and second-round exits. By the time the 1999–2000 season rolled around, the Devils' trap system had been written off as flawed, given that they had failed to make it back into the finals since their win in 1995. The Devils still had a dominant defensive core, but they could not put the shots in the net that were required to win games. Going into the 2000 post-season, every sports writer expected the trap system to fail again, leading to another early exit from the playoffs. But the Devils never paid any attention to what sports writers said and played their game the way their coach wanted. Now led by Hall of Fame defenseman Larry Robinson, the Devils easily handed the Florida Panthers their walking papers and took the fight to the second round against the Toronto Maple Leafs.

As smooth as the series against Florida had gone for the Devils, it hadn't been that easy for Niedermayer. Florida's Peter Worrell was widely known throughout the league as one of the toughest guys on the ice, and during an early games against the Devils, he made it his mission to pound the New Jersey defense into submission. After repeated rough checks from Worrell, Niedermayer became increasingly frustrated with his treatment during the game and with the referee's unwillingness to put a stop to it. Worrell was checking Niedermayer hard in the corner of the rink when the two players started pushing and shoving. Niedermayer thought Worrell had pushed one too many times and turned around and used his stick to smack the top of Worrell's helmet. As soon as Niedermayer hit Worrell with his stick, he knew he had gone too far. The referee broke up the players, and Niedermayer was thrown out of the game and given a one-game suspension.

When the Devils eliminated the Panthers, Niedermayer nervously approached Worrell to shake his hand. "When we were shaking hands with the other team, I basically left it up to him. If he was willing to shake my hand, I was willing to shake his. I was willing to put it behind me. I wasn't proud of what happened, and I left it up to him to shake my hand. He did, so that's the end of it, hopefully," said Niedermayer later in the playoffs about the incident.

The series against Toronto was going to be defense versus offense, and it was anyone's guess as to who would come out the victor. After splitting the first two games with the Leafs, the Devils easily beat them in game three by a score of 5–1, and, with that, it looked like New Jersey had turned the series in their favor. Niedermayer was asked if the Leafs looked a little shaken after the game. "Well, last night they did a bit, definitely. We still have two more wins to get in this playoff series. If we don't do that, last night was worth nothing." Toronto came back and won game four to tie the series, but the crushing blow in game three had sealed the Leafs' fate.

The Devils moved on to face the Philadelphia Flyers in the conference finals. The Flyers proved to be harder opponents than the Leafs: they battled hard in every game, and when it looked like they were down, they would bounce back with a flurry of goals. The series was a tight affair, with the Flyers making Niedermayer's job difficult. The Flyers took the early lead in the series, up 2–1, but the Devils never gave up and fought back to win it in seven games.

Back in finals again, Niedermayer was asked to compare this Devils team with the one that won the Cup in 1995. "We're definitely a really good team, up with the top teams in the NHL. Obviously, the 1995 team, when you win the Stanley Cup, there's no team better than you, and we still have a ways to go to get there. Similarities would be, obviously with Marty Brodeur in net, that's one. There were a few guys back here in '95 who know what it takes to go all the way. We also have some new guys who are excited to be here and excited to be in the playoffs, so I think it's a good mix."

It was the perfect mix. The Devils tightened up defensively for the match-up against the Dallas Stars, and after game one, which they won 7–3, it was clear to many people which team would win the Stanley Cup. The Devils dominated, and Niedermayer won his second Stanley Cup. He had contributed with 5 goals and 2 assists, 2 of his goals coming shorthanded.

The Devils made it back into the finals the following season, silencing any critics who said the team was the product of a boring defensive system. You simply could not argue with the Devils' production. Unfortunately for Niedermayer, the Devils could not defeat the Colorado Avalanche in the 2001 Stanley Cup finals, losing in the seventh game. But just two years later, the Devils would again take the Stanley Cup.

In 2002, Niedermayer joined Team Canada in their bid to bring home Olympic gold in hockey for the first time in 50 years. Able to use his lightning speed on the larger ice surface of international rinks, Niedermayer was by far one of the best defensemen in the tournament, helping Canada past Finland, Belarus and the United States to win the gold.

After three Stanley Cups, several All-Star games and an Olympic gold medal, there was no doubt that Niedermayer was one of the best defensemen in the NHL and would one day end up in the Hockey Hall of Fame. But Niedermayer was not finished with collecting praise. After the 2003–04 season, in which he was named captain of the New Jersey Devils after the retirement of fellow blueliner Scott Stevens, Niedermayer ended the year with a career high of 14 goals, 40 assists and a plus/minus rating of +20. His contribution to his team and his commitment to his game earned him the Norris Trophy as the best defenseman in the league, finally breaking Nicklas Lidstrom's three-year reign.

In August 2005, Scott Niedermayer's long journey with the New Jersey Devils came to an end when he joined his brother, Rob, and the Anaheim Ducks, signing a four-year, $27-million contract. Scott fit perfectly in the Western Conference, which is has traditionally been more centered around the offensive aspects of the game. With the Ducks, Niedermayer could now feel free to use his speed, and in his first season in

Anaheim, he had a career year with 13 goals and 50 assists, for 63 points.

In the 2006–07 season, he improved upon the previous one with 15 goals and 54 assists, for a career high of 69 points. Niedermayer, joining up with Chris Pronger, formed one of the best defensive combinations in the league, making it likely that the Ducks would go far in the playoffs with two of the best blueliners. "We sort of complement each other on what we're able to do, what we bring to a situation like that. It's been easy and fun," Niedermayer said about Pronger in an interview with *The Hockey News*.

Pronger returned the kind words to his defensive partner: "We're able to learn from each other in practice, and throughout the course of the games, being able to play with a player of Scott's caliber and character certainly is something that not only I but our whole team can learn from."

In the playoffs, Niedermayer performed his usual magic on the ice, helping the Ducks breeze past the first few rounds. The Ducks seemed to have no problem in each round, coolly dispensing of each challenger in no more than six games. Niedermayer performed his duties like a true quality defenseman: no one really notices his presence on the ice, but once he steps off, his contribution to the team becomes abundantly clear.

With two Norris Trophy–winning defensemen on the Ducks team, it wasn't surprising to watch them make it into the Stanley Cup finals against the Ottawa Senators. Led by Niedermayer, the Ducks were clearly the better team and defeated the Sens in five games. For his effort and qualities as a leader, Niedermayer was awarded the Conn Smythe Trophy as the playoffs' Most Valuable Player. In an interview after the victory, Niedermayer was overly humble about his contribution to the team's victory. "I was a little surprised," he said. "We had a handful of candidates I think. I was out there trying to do my thing. To be recognized like that, I'm thankful."

If the Ducks can keep the nucleus of their Stanley Cup–winning blue line, then they will be the favorites next season to repeat as champions and possibly bring back the era of the dynasties. And if things continue with the same upward momentum for Niedermayer that has characterized most of his career, he will certainly have a spot in the Hockey Hall of Fame as one of most well-rounded players ever to play his position.

Season	Team	GP	Goals	Assists	Points	+/–	Penalties
1991–92	New Jersey	4	0	1	1	1	2
1992–93	New Jersey	80	11	29	40	8	47
1993–94	New Jersey	81	10	36	46	34	42
1994–95	New Jersey	48	4	15	19	19	18
1995–96	New Jersey	79	8	25	33	5	46
1996–97	New Jersey	81	5	30	35	–4	64
1997–98	New Jersey	81	14	43	57	5	27
1998–99	New Jersey	72	11	35	46	16	26
1999–2000	New Jersey	71	7	31	38	19	48
2000–01	New Jersey	57	6	29	35	14	22
2001–02	New Jersey	76	11	22	33	12	30
2002–03	New Jersey	81	11	28	39	23	62
2003–04	New Jersey	81	14	40	54	20	44
2005–06	Anaheim	82	13	50	63	8	96
2006–07	Anaheim	79	15	54	69	8	86

Chapter Three

Brian Rafalski

Underestimated, Never Overrated

Not all paths to the National Hockey League take the same route. Most players are drafted in their junior years, and if they are good enough, they are given a shot with their pro team. But sometimes, a team just doesn't have enough space, and that player gets lost in the hockey system. It's hard to believe when you see Brian Rafalski play the game today that his path to the NHL was less than smooth.

At five feet, ten inches tall, Rafalski wasn't one of the biggest defensemen, but he made up for his shortcomings with his excellent speed and puck-handling skills. He entered the U.S. college hockey system with the University of Wisconsin Badgers and was one of the better players on the team. In his senior year with the team, he scored 11 goals and 34 assists and hoped that his performance was good enough for one of the NHL clubs to notice him. He was the standout player in the National Collegiate Athletic Association men's ice hockey tournament, and he lead the Badgers to the championship.

But after graduating in 1995 without any interest from a major league team, Rafalski was not about to give up on his dream of playing professional hockey. The next available route for the 22-year-old college graduate was to play in Europe because it offered a competitive challenge and was a good place to display his skills, given his smaller size. If there was any league in which he was likely to get noticed by NHL scouts, it was in Europe, where scouts were showing an ever-increasing interest in European talent.

Rafalski started out his European career in the Swedish Elite League, but it wasn't until he moved to Finland and played in the SM-Liiga, where his skills were finally noticed. By his fifth year playing in the European system, Rafalski was evolving into one of the best players without an NHL contract. In the 1998–99 SM-Liiga season, he scored 19 goals and 34 assists and was given the Kultainen Kypara, which is awarded to the best player in the league as voted by his peers. It was the first time in the trophy's history that it was given to a non-Finnish player. In 1999, the sports journal *Sporting News* named him as one of the best players in the world not playing in the NHL. All the praise finally got the attention of the New Jersey Devils, who signed him before any other teams got wind of his talent. Finally, at the age of 26, Rafalski realized his dream of playing in the National Hockey League.

In the 1999–2000 NHL season, Rafalski had less room to use his superior skating skills and focused mainly on being a reliable positional defenseman. During his rookie year, he scored only 5 goals and 27 assists, but more telling of his success was his plus/minus rating of +21. With Rafalski on the Devils' side, along with fellow defensemen Scott Stevens, Scott Niedermayer and Ken Daneyko, the Devils defense was nearly impenetrable. Rafalski was a major contributor in the Devils' run to the Stanley Cup and provided a key insurance goal in game four of the finals against the Dallas Stars, which ended in a close 3–1 victory. All those years of uncertainty and waiting faded away once he got to lift the Stanley Cup above his head.

Not a bad rookie season. Scouts who had overlooked him for the bigger defensemen were now left scratching their heads, trying to figure out how they missed out on a quality player whose skills were there from the beginning. He may be small for what is considered a normal defenseman in the NHL, but he more than made up for it with his puck-handling skills, his incredible strength in the corners and in front of the net and a work ethic that rivaled most on his team.

Although he had accomplished his goal of making it to the NHL and winning the Stanley Cup, Rafalski still had to prove to himself that he could be one of the best players in the league. In addition, as many Stanley Cup champions will attest to, once you win one, you want another. In his sophomore season, Rafalski improved his stats with 9 goals and 43 assists and was the most valuable player in the Devils' post-season as they pushed for their second straight Stanley Cup. He was instrumental not only on defense during the post-season, but also in his contribution to the offense. Three of his 7 goals were game winners, and he assisted on 11 others. But his offensive output could not win all the games, and despite a valiant effort by the Devils in making it into the finals, they were defeated by the Colorado Avalanche.

Undeterred, Rafalski returned for the 2001–02 season and added to his long list of accomplishments when he was selected to appear in the NHL All-Star game, but he was forced to sit out because of an injury. When it came time for the U.S. Olympic hockey team to select its players, he was at the top of their list. During the Olympics, he scored only 1 goal but was solid on the U.S. blue line, quarterbacking many of the American rushes. He left the Olympics with a silver medal and returned to the Devils lineup to complete a good season, but the team was eliminated by the Carolina Hurricanes in the first round of the playoffs.

Rafalski would be the first to admit that it takes hard work to get into the Stanley Cup playoffs, but that every victory takes a little bit of luck, too. After all, Rafalski had been in the NHL just three seasons and had already won a Stanley Cup, an invitation to the All-Star game and an Olympic silver medal with the U.S. national hockey team. With a little luck and a lot of hard work, Rafalski and the Devils found themselves in a good position going into the 2003 playoffs with the fourth best record during the regular season. The Devils made it past the Boston Bruins and the Tampa Bay Lightning and had a difficult time with the Ottawa Senators before making it once again into the finals, this time against the Anaheim Mighty Ducks. Rafalski contributed 2 goals and 9 assists in the Devils' run to another Stanley Cup.

Many teams have shown interest in acquiring Rafalski, but the Devils know talent when they see it. Although he is now 33 years old, there are still a few good years of hockey left in his legs. With 55 points for the 2006–07 NHL season, a career best, Rafalski has proven the saying that sometimes, things only get better with age.

Season	Team	GP	Goals	Assists	Points	+/-	Penalties
1999–2000	New Jersey	75	5	27	32	21	28
2000–01	New Jersey	78	9	43	52	36	26
2001–02	New Jersey	76	7	40	47	15	18
2002–03	New Jersey	79	3	37	40	18	14
2003–04	New Jersey	69	6	30	36	6	24
2005–06	New Jersey	82	6	43	49	0	36
2006–07	New Jersey	82	8	47	55	4	34

Chapter Four

Tomas Kaberle

From Humble Beginnings

As hockey has grown in popularity around the world, it's no longer just Canadian kids who grow up shooting pucks on a local frozen pond or under the dim light of a street lamp. Hockey is particularly popular in the eastern European countries, where kids today grow up worshipping players like Jari Kurri, Sergei Fedorov and Wayne Gretzky (hockey perfection knows no nationality), and excellent youth hockey programs get kids involved in the sport at an early age.

Growing up in the Czech Republic, Tomas Kaberle enjoyed watching hockey games when he could, but he got his inspiration from his father, who played for the Czechoslovakian national team in the 1970s, winning a bronze medal in 1972 and silver in 1976. As a young Kaberle progressed through the Czech youth hockey system, his father was always at the arena to support his son and give him pointers when he needed them. A large kid early on, Kaberle gravitated toward the defensive spot because he had worked hard on his skating and found that he had a booming slap shot that served him well from the point. Ever since the early days, he has remained on the blue line.

Although Kaberle was a good player, his talent was passed over for a number of years because his size—six feet, two inches tall and 200 pounds—was often considered to impede his progress in the faster and larger ice surfaces of Europe. He finally got signed with Kladno, a reputable team in the Czech Extraliga, at the age of 16, but he wasn't used very often in his first two years. The coaches knew he was good, but they felt he still had some maturing to do when it came to his ability to read how a play would develop on the ice. That ability is one of the most important parts of the game for any young defenseman to learn, and the most difficult. If a player can see foresee how and where the opposing players will break out of their zone, then he can anticipate and stop the play.

Kaberle had difficulty adapting his style to the new coaches' needs. In his first two seasons with Kladno, he was dressed for only 27 games and saw limited ice time. But he did not let that deter him. Kaberle worked even harder on his game, getting the occasional tip from his father on fine-tuning the smaller aspects of his game. By the end of the 1995–96 Extraliga season, Kaberle had earned the trust of the coach and was given the opportunity to play in a few playoff games. It was the boost he needed to step up his game.

During the summer of 1996, Kaberle was surprised that he was eligible for the NHL entry draft but had little faith that he would be selected by any team because he didn't think he had played enough games to show the scouts what he could contribute to a team. As the draft progressed through the first round, then the second, third, fourth, fifth, sixth and seventh, Kaberle was sure that the opportunity to play in the NHL would pass him by. Most players who are selected in the late rounds never actually get to play for the team that drafted them, and he almost preferred that he wouldn't be selected so he could return to his team, play a full season and prove himself worthy. But the Toronto Maple Leafs saw something in his game and his character that they liked and selected him in the eighth and final round, 204th overall.

After his selection, Kaberle spent two more seasons with Kladno, where his game experience and ice time increased after being drafted by the Maple Leafs. The coaches thought that if Toronto saw something in the young defenseman, then they may as well use him in regular games. Although Kaberle did not often contribute on the scoreboard, finally scoring his first goal in his last season in the Extraliga, his defensive skills were finally up to standard and, in his final year, far above most of the other defensemen in the league. In 1998, Leafs management thought Kaberle was ready to come to North America to join the American Hockey League's St. John's Maple Leafs for a few games of conditioning before getting his first shot in the NHL.

Before the 1998–99 pre-season preparations, Kaberle impressed head coach Pat Quinn enough to earn a shot in the lineup during the regular season. In the first game of the season, Quinn wanted to test the rookie's fitness and had him on the ice for a full 29 minutes in a 2–1 win over the defending Stanley Cup champions, the Detroit Red Wings. The North American game seemed to suit Kaberle's style better than the European, and, under the watchful eye of Quinn, he quickly developed into one of the better defensemen on the team. Coming seemingly out of nowhere, he put in a valiant effort in the 57 games he played, scoring 4 goals and 18 assists and earning a plus/minus rating of +3. By the next season, he had earned a regular spot on the Leafs' blue line and has been their top defenseman since.

For the 1999–2000 season, the Maple Leafs were looking to implement a faster system of moving the puck up the ice, and Kaberle's skill and poise with the puck suited the new system perfectly. After an injury to Leafs defenseman Bryan Berard, Kaberle was moved up in the lineup and did not disappoint in all the 82 games he played during the season. He scored 7 goals and 33 assists, for 40 points, and showed increasing ability in his skating and moving the puck out of the Leafs' zone with accurate tape-to-tape passes. The Leafs were happy with his progress, especially because he came out of nowhere and was making only $250,000 a year. Kaberle's shot from the point, excellent vision of the ice and sharp sense of when to join the rush or hang back made him, along with Bryan McCabe, one of the two defensemen Quinn would look to on the power play.

Over the next few seasons, Kaberle improved his numbers and became a fixture in the Leafs' lineup. Other teams began to recognize what Kaberle had to offer, and Leafs management began to get tempting trade offers from other teams. During the 2000–01 season, the Leafs received an offer from the Philadelphia Flyers to trade Kaberle for the often-injured but highly useful Eric Lindros. Given Kaberle's importance to the Leafs' defense and the Philadelphia superstar's habit of getting injured, it did not take long for the Leafs to respond to the offer with a solid "No, thank you!" The non-deal was highly criticized in the media, but the Leafs would not deal a player who could make up the core of their defense for years to come for a player who was known for his mood swings and susceptibility to injury.

In the 2001–02 campaign, Kaberle was selected to the World team for the All-Star game and received further praise for his game when the Czech national team came calling for the 2002 Olympics. His team did not come away from the Olympics with any medals, but the experience definitely improved Kaberle's game. In the 2002 playoffs, the Leafs were in a good position to go far after eliminating the New York Islanders in the first round and the speedy, high-scoring Ottawa Senators in the second. But the Leafs have had trouble making it to the finals since their last appearance in 1967. Despite Kaberle's contribution of 2 goals and 8 assists, the Leafs could not rise above their history and were defeated in the conference finals by the Carolina Hurricanes. In 2002–03, Kaberle had a career year with 11 goals, 36 assists and a plus/minus rating of +20, but the Philadelphia Flyers cut his playoff hopes short in the first round with a game seven 6–1 victory over the Leafs.

Kaberle was a solid presence on the Leafs' blue line, and his aspirations to make it deep into the playoffs never changed, but the team around him just hadn't been able to make it past the first round since 2003, or even into the playoffs in 2005–2006 or 2006–2007. Despite the losses, Kaberle continued to believe in his team, which is why, in February 2006, he signed a five-year contract worth $21.2 million through to the 2010–11 season.

In March 2007, Kaberle received the scare of his career while playing the New Jersey Devils. As Kaberle was clearing the puck from his zone, he took his eye off the play for one moment, and Devils tough guy Cam Janssen came swooping in with a late hit that caught Kaberle in the head and knocked him to the ice, where he lay unconscious. The stretcher was called for, and Kaberle was removed from the ice and sent immediately to the local hospital. It turned out to be a concussion and forced him to miss out on an important eight games: the Leafs were trying to secure a playoff spot and could have used his help. Janssen was given a three-game suspension but never once apologized for the late hit.

Leafs general manager John Ferguson commented on the hit after the game. "In instances like this, it might make sense if the player is suspended indefinitely until you get more information back on the extent of the injury," he said. "That's one way you could address the situation. We know this is a dangerous game...a physical game, a speed game. But there are lines that shouldn't be crossed."

Kaberle had nothing but contempt for Janssen. "I don't care [to hear from him]. He doesn't respect me and I don't respect him."

Kaberle eventually recovered and returned in time to help the Leafs in their push to make the playoffs, but the team missed out on the final playoff spot by one point. Despite the disappointing end to the season, Toronto fans know that Kaberle will be back next season to take his spot on the blue line as one of the top d-men on the team.

Season	Team	GP	Goals	Assists	Points	+/-	Penalties
1998–99	Toronto	57	4	18	22	3	12
1999–2000	Toronto	82	7	33	40	3	24
2000–01	Toronto	82	6	39	45	10	24
2001–02	Toronto	69	10	29	39	5	2
2002–03	Toronto	82	11	36	47	20	30
2003–04	Toronto	71	3	28	31	16	18
2005–06	Toronto	82	9	58	67	–1	46
2006–07	Toronto	74	11	47	58	3	20

Chapter Five

Bryan McCabe

The Clutch Defenseman

This native of St. Catharines, Ontario, began playing hockey at an early age and knew he wanted to be a professional hockey player the moment he played in his first organized game. As he rose through the ranks of the Canadian hockey system, a young Bryan McCabe gravitated toward playing defense because he was one of the better skaters among kids his age and had a powerful shot from the point. He has always been more of an offensive defenseman, but he never neglects his duties on the line, making him one of the best in the league today.

McCabe started off on his path to the National Hockey League in the juniors with the Western Hockey League's Medicine Hat Tigers. Alberta was a long way from his hometown in Ontario, but McCabe knew that countless other professionals before him had to make the same sacrifice to realize their dreams of playing in the

NHL. That isn't to say, however, that it wasn't difficult for the 16-year-old defenseman. To keep his mind off the separation from his family, McCabe focused on his game, and in his first season with the Tigers, he impressed everyone with a very aggressive style of play. In 68 games during the 1991–92 season, he scored 6 goals, got 24 assists and racked up over 150 minutes in penalties.

McCabe started out the 1992–93 season with the Tigers but was traded halfway through to the Spokane Chiefs. He played another season of rough-and-tumble hockey, scoring just 3 goals in 46 games but managing to earn 134 minutes in penalties. His offensive edge and his aggressive play helped him gain some attention from NHL scouts before the 1993 entry draft, mostly from the New York Islanders. The Islanders were building a base of young, talented players and thought that McCabe's physical, offensive style would fit perfectly into their organization. McCabe was drafted 40th overall and returned to the WHL to prove to his NHL affiliate that he belonged in the pros.

During the 1993–94 season with the Chiefs, McCabe exploded with one of the most offensive seasons of his career, scoring 22 goals and 62 assists. Despite the amazing numbers he put up,

McCabe was then sent off to the Brandon Wheat Kings for the 1994–95 season, where he helped the team into the playoff finals, only to lose to the Kamloops Blazers in six games.

The regular season disappointments did little to keep McCabe down. On the international stage, McCabe and the Canadian junior team dominated the World Junior Championship in 1994 and 1995. His solid defensive skills and fast skating were a key ingredient in Canada's success in bringing home the gold both times. After the World Juniors in 1995, where he scored 3 goals and 9 assists, the New York Islanders knew that McCabe, now 20 years old, was mature enough to make the jump to the National Hockey League.

McCabe's first season with the Islanders was a mediocre affair: he scored only 7 goals and 16 assists in the full 82-game schedule. The Islanders, however, were less than mediocre, and if it weren't for the expansion Ottawa Senators and the San Jose Sharks, the Islanders would have garnered the dubious honor of the worst team in the NHL during the 1995–96 season. McCabe spent another two years with the Islanders, doing his best to stem the tide of losses, and for trying to keep the team together, he was given the captaincy before the start of the 1997–98 season. At 22 years old, McCabe found himself in a position normally reserved for seasoned veterans, but the Islanders were trading players so often that McCabe ended up as the top selection. But the honor would not last long: McCabe himself became a victim of the Islanders' desperate search for team chemistry, and he was traded to the Vancouver Canucks mid-season. He spent just one and half seasons with the Canucks before another trade to the dismal Chicago Blackhawks, and he soon packed his bags again when the Hawks sent him off to the Toronto Maple Leafs. The Maple Leafs weren't prepared to give Alexander Karpovtsev the lucrative contract he was looking for, and they saw the perfect opportunity to get a young, undervalued defenseman in McCabe while clearing up some funds.

In Toronto, under the watchful eye of head coach Pat Quinn, McCabe flourished into the dominant player he was in the juniors, adding that extra offensive touch that the Leafs were looking for. Joining Kaberle on the Maple Leafs' blue line, McCabe added an extra touch of grit to a team long criticized for folding under the pressure of a physical game. After a solid first season from McCabe, the Maple Leafs were assured that he would be part of a winning combination for the franchise. During the 2001 playoffs, McCabe played well as the Leafs handed a crushing defeat to the Ottawa Senators in the first round, before being knocked out by the Devils in a close series that took a full seven games to finish. McCabe rebounded from the 2001 playoff loss with 17 goals and 26 assists in the 2001–02 season, finally being recognized as one of the top defensemen in the league.

Realizing his importance to the team, McCabe made an effort to curb his sinful ways so he wouldn't have to spend so much time in the penalty box. This growing maturity could be seen in his game, with a career-high plus/minus rating of +22 for the 2003–04 season. He became the defenseman of choice, along with partner Tomas Kaberle, for the Leafs' power play attack, and his blast from the point earned the respect of goaltenders throughout the league. Whenever the Leafs were down by a goal with a few minutes left in the game, without a doubt, McCabe would be on the point blasting in one of his patented low slap shots to get the last-minute equalizer or game winner.

McCabe had the best year of his career in 2005–06, scoring 19 goals and 49 assists, but all those goals could not help get the Leafs into the playoffs. For the first time in four years, McCabe was forced to watch the post-season from the golf clubhouse. This was also the year that Leafs management would have to decide if it was worth paying McCabe the salary that a top defenseman earns in the NHL. As an unrestricted free agent, McCabe was at liberty to take any qualifying offers from other teams, but he hesitated to sign any contracts that summer because he found out his wife needed major surgery and felt that family comes first. He didn't want to think about business when his wife needed him. McCabe finally decided to stay on with the Leafs, signing a five-year, $28.75-million contract.

Toronto media were ruthless in their treatment of McCabe for putting off the signing, and during a press conference, he set the record straight. "[Roberta] was scheduled to undergo major surgery June 22 and I didn't feel it was appropriate to sign until I knew everything was in order," he said, fighting back tears. "So I put it on hold. Meanwhile, all these reports going around were erroneous and disappointing. No one knows what my family has gone through recently, but at least my wife is on the road to recovery. It's very difficult to deal with these issues while your family is being ripped in the press."

Back with the Leafs for the 2006–07 season, McCabe put aside all the problems that occurred during the summer and got back to the game he loved. Despite his 15 goals and 42 assists, the Leafs still missed out on the playoffs, but there is no doubt that McCabe will be right back on the Leafs' blue line next season, quarterbacking the team to future success.

Season	Team	GP	Goals	Assists	Points	+/-	Penalties
1995–96	NY Islanders	82	4	16	23	–24	156
1996–97	NY Islanders	82	4	20	28	–2	165
1997–98	NY Islanders	56	4	9	12	9	145
1997–98	Vancouver	26	4	11	12	10	64
1998–99	Vancouver	69	4	14	21	–11	120
1999–2000	Chicago	79	7	19	25	–8	139
2000–01	Toronto	82	6	24	29	16	123
2001–02	Toronto	82	10	26	43	16	129
2002–03	Toronto	75	11	18	24	9	135
2003–04	Toronto	75	3	37	53	22	86
2005–06	Toronto	73	9	49	68	–1	116
2006–07	Toronto	82	11	42	57	3	115

Chapter Six

Zdeno Chara

Goliath on Skates

When hockey fans got their first look at Zdeno Chara, they thought he had wandered into the wrong sport. At six feet, nine inches tall, Chara looked like he belonged in the National Basketball Association rather than on the ice with an NHL team, where the average height of most hockey players is six feet, two inches. His height did not necessarily translate into an advantage for Chara when it came to his hockey career. Considered more of a novelty act than a serious hockey player, he was underestimated by many people who considered him to be good for clearing opponents out of the goal crease, but not much more. But Chara was not raised to give up, and never once did he doubt that he could make it as one of the best d-men in the league.

He was born in the little Slovakian town of Trencin on March 18, 1977, to Zdenek and Viktoria

Chara. His father, at six feet, two inches, and his mother, at five feet, nine inches, were not small by any measure, and as little Zdeno got older, he quickly grew taller than his friends. He was drawn to sports early on. His father had represented Czechoslovakia in the 1976 Summer Olympic Games as a Greco-Roman wrestler, and he wanted to follow in his athletic father's footsteps.

Under his father's strict supervision, young Chara was put on a strict regimen of physical training that strained the teenager close to the breaking point. "Many times, he pushed me so hard that I ended up crying. I would wonder why he was so mean to me, but I didn't understand what he was trying to do. He meant it in a good way," said Chara, looking back on his formative years.

All the training and preparations began to bear fruit for Chara as he excelled in all the sports he tried, but he found he had a true passion for hockey. There was just one problem: at 16 years old, Chara was already six feet, six inches tall, and his hockey coaches had no idea how to handle such a player when the rest of the team were all just pushing six feet. His father remembered one instance when his son showed concern over his ever-increasing height: "I remember one night he called me into his room and told me that he could feel his thighs growing."

His first few years in hockey in the European system were difficult for the awkward teenager because on the larger ice surface, it was difficult for him to keep up with the speedier, smaller players. Coaches and friends urged Chara to take up a sport more fitting of his stature, such as basketball, but when he pulled down the rim while dunking the ball, he was banned from returning. That didn't bother Chara, though, because it was hockey he wanted to play. At 17 years old and towering at an amazing six feet, nine inches, Chara was playing Junior B hockey, but when you out-size the other players by nearly a foot, it can be hard to find proper-fitting equipment. Since he wasn't considered a priority on the team, he was forced to squeeze into shoulder and shin pads way too small for him, and he had to play on a pair of skates that were falling apart. But Chara persevered through the adversity and was then able to realize why his father had pushed him so hard.

Chara wasn't the best skater or the defenseman with the best vision on the ice, but his height was a definite bonus to NHL teams looking for a big man to clear out space in front of their nets. At the 1996 entry draft, while smaller, more mobile defensemen were being selected, the New York Islanders kept a watchful eye on Chara. The Islanders were in need of a physical presence on their blue line after several seasons spent in the basement of the league. Chara was over seven feet tall with skates on, so the Islanders decided to give the big man a try and selected him 56th overall. The relatively high selection surprised Chara, who was used to being disregarded as a mere commodity rather than valued as a serious hockey player who could contribute to a team.

Chara did not want to let the opportunity to play in the NHL pass him by, so he picked up his belongings and moved to Canada to play in the Western Hockey League with the Prince George Cougars. "If I had stayed in Slovakia, I probably wouldn't be playing hockey today, I'm sure. It was probably the best thing that happened to me," said Chara years later about the decision.

If he had stayed in the Slovakian league with Dukla Trencin, he would have continued to be underused by the coaches, who could not use his size properly on the larger ice surface. But now with the Cougars on smaller North American ice surfaces, Chara's full potential became easy to see for the team that took a chance on him in the draft. In the WHL, Chara was an obvious attraction for fans and an obvious worry for opponents. On the larger European surfaces, forwards could skate around Chara when entering his defensive zone, but on the smaller surface, Chara had the advantage of choosing whether to take the puck or drill the player into the boards. Any player who dared challenge him learned quickly that it wasn't so easy to get physical with the giant of a man, and when a player did challenge him and a fight broke out, it was Chara again with the advantage. With his amazing reach and power, his opponents usually ended up on the ice covering their heads as he tossed them around like crash test dummies.

After spending a little over one season in the minors, the New York Islanders finally called Chara up to the NHL to play his first game on November 19, 1997, in Detroit against the Red Wings. He got to play in only 25 games that season, recording only 1 assist, but the experience was valuable to the young player, who was eager to learn all he could about the North American professional game. The Islanders wanted Chara to keep his game simple, using him sparingly on power plays and keeping him well back of the play to protect the defense against any odd-man rushes. Chara did not mind the overly defensive roll he was assigned, and his ability to see how a play would develop improved considerably. He was earning over 15 minutes of ice time per game, and by the end of his first full year, 1998–99, he was the team leader in hits and shots blocked. But because Chara was continually used on the penalty-killing unit, his plus/minus rating suffered: after the 1999–2000 season, his rating had plummeted to –27.

Despite the less-than-perfect statistics, Chara improved considerably in his first three seasons in the National Hockey League, enough to finally be invited to join the Slovakian national hockey team for the 2000 World Championship. Chara helped the tiny country surpass great hockey nations like Canada and Russia to take home the silver medal in a heart-wrenching loss to former countrymen, the Czech Republic.

Chara returned to the NHL for his third full season of hockey and was more confident than ever in his developing skills. He still did not mind following the Islanders' system and having to sit back on defense, but inside he was craving a chance to take his game to another level. He played in all 82 of the Islanders games that year and became the NHL's top checker, delivering 373 bone crunching hits, but another plus/minus rating of –27 worried the Islanders management, who wanted to add a scoring touch to their struggling team.

During the 2001 entry draft, the Ottawa Senators wanted desperately to get their hands on top prospect Jason Spezza, but the New York Islanders had the privilege of holding that selection. Knowing that the Islanders wanted a scoring forward, and given their continual contract disputes with Alexei Yashin, the Senators offered up Yashin in return for the Islanders' second pick (which they used to get Jason Spezza), along with Zdeno Chara and Bill Mucklat. The Islanders were happy with Yashin, and the Senators could barely believe their luck in landing such a great deal.

Chara was not aware of it at the time, but his trade to the Senators would be the second best move of his as-yet-brief professional career. The Senators had strung together a series of successful seasons, but they were widely seen as a soft team when it came down to the grind of the playoffs. A man of Chara's stature fit into the style of play the Senators were trying to accomplish, all while keeping that offensive edge.

New teammate and childhood friend Marian Hossa (who was a Senator in 2001 when Chara joined the team) was excited to have the big guy on his side for once, remembering all those times back in Trencin when he would go to the net and get knocked to the ice by the Goliath standing in front of the net. "I'm a lot happier that he's on my team," said Hossa after the trade. "I've talked to Marty [Havlat] and Radek [Bonk] and they're pleased they don't have to go against him anymore." (Both Havlat and Bonk were with the Senators at the time but are now with other teams.)

Chara knew that the Senators had acquired him for his obvious physical talents, but head coach Jacques Martin knew that the big defenseman could be more useful. Chara made the perfect screen in front of goaltenders when Ottawa was on the power play, and on his first try in front of the net, he scored a goal to end a five-game string, during which Ottawa had been one for 17 with the man advantage. With the Senators, Chara grew into the player he had always wanted to become: a dominating physical presence on the ice and an occasional contributor to the offense. In his first season with Ottawa, he scored 10 goals and 13 assists and improved his plus/minus rating from a horrible –27 with the Islanders to +30 with the Senators. It was beginning to look like the Islanders had made a big mistake in letting Chara go so easily.

On the international scene, as Chara's other teammates prepared for the upcoming 2002 Winter Olympics, the Slovakian team was forced to play in a qualifying tournament just to make it into the games. Canada, Russia, Sweden and others were automatically in the final tournament held during the games, which the NHL gave its players permission to play in, but NHL players did not have permission to play in the preliminary tournament. This meant that players such as Hossa and Chara could not play in all their country's games to help them into the Olympics. Slovakia had to sit out, and a disappointed Chara returned to Canada.

Chara helped Ottawa to get into the 2001–02 post-season and was instrumental in stopping the Philadelphia Flyers' attack in the first round of the playoffs, during which the Senators defeated them in five games. Philadelphia Flyer Jeremy Roenick, known for his off-the-cuff remarks, commented on the big Ottawa defenseman: "Oh my God, with his wingspan and size, it's like he's 13 feet long."

But in the second round, the Senators came up against the Toronto Maple Leafs and were embroiled in one of the fastest growing rivalries in hockey. Chara was on top of the world, being in the first playoffs of his career, and wanted to give everything he had to take Ottawa into the finals. Toronto and Ottawa split the first four games and went into the crucial fifth game hoping to avoid giving the other team the advantage in game six. With eight minutes to play in the third period and the score tied at 2 goals apiece, the Senators were fiercely trying to keep the puck in the Leafs' zone when Chara tried to pinch in to stop it from getting out. But when he missed the puck, he left himself vulnerable to a hit, and that's exactly when Leafs forward Alyn McCauley hit him with enough force to send the giant to the ice in obvious pain. Chara was helped off the ice and did not return to finish out the game; in fact, he would not return at all that season. After a lengthy examination from team doctors, it turned out Chara had a strained medial collateral ligament. Without the big man on the line, the Senators could not match the Leafs' physical play and lost the series in the seventh game by a score of 3–0.

After suffering through his country's loss in the Olympic preliminaries, the Senators' early exit from the 2002 playoffs, and then a heartbreaking loss to the New Jersey Devils in game seven of the 2003 conference finals, Chara returned to training camp for the 2003–04 season more determined than ever. In the 79 regular-season games Chara played in, he scored a career high of 16 goals, assisted on 25 others and achieved a career-high plus/minus rating of +33. Chara knew he had finally arrived in the NHL when he was recommended for the Norris Trophy as best defenseman in the league, but he just missed out to the New Jersey Devils' Scott Niedermayer.

When the playoffs began, the Senators yet again met up against the Toronto Maple Leafs, and again they were eliminated prematurely in the first round. Frustration began to set in. After seven years of leading the Senators from the basement of the NHL to the top in the regular season, head coach Jacques Martin was fired and replaced by coaching veteran Bryan Murray. Chara had another good season in 2005–06, scoring 16 goals and 27 assists, and so did the Senators, who looked confident and poised to make a serious run in the playoffs with new additions such as sniper Dany Heatley. The Senators could relax a little knowing they were not going to face the Maple Leafs in the playoffs because the Leafs simply did not have enough points to make the post-season after a disappointing regular season. The Senators instead met the defending Stanley Cup champions, the Tampa Bay Lightning, in the first round and defeated them in five games. But when confronted with a more serious challenge from the young and speedy Buffalo Sabres, Ottawa once again found themselves on the golf course way too early in the post-season.

In the off-season, now as an unrestricted free agent, Chara wanted a change of scenery and a team to which he could contribute not just as a player but also as a leader. On July 1, 2006, he signed a five-year, $37.5-million contract with the Boston Bruins, and just before the season got underway, he was named the team's captain. As much as Chara relished his role on his new team, the Bruins had a terrible year, finishing out of the playoffs, while Chara's numbers suffered as well. With a plus/minus rating of –21, he was negative for the first time since leaving the Islanders.

Despite the bad season, Chara has come a long way from the awkward giant who could barely skate to one of the premier defensemen in the league. But he would surely tell everyone that he never doubted himself for a moment.

Season	Team	GP	Goals	Assists	Points	+/-	Penalties
1997–98	NY Islanders	25	0	1	1	1	50
1998–99	NY Islanders	59	2	6	8	–8	83
1999–2000	NY Islanders	65	2	9	11	–27	57
2000–01	NY Islanders	82	2	7	9	–27	157
2001–02	Ottawa	75	10	13	23	30	156
2002–03	Ottawa	74	9	30	39	29	116
2003–04	Ottawa	79	16	25	41	33	147
2005–06	Ottawa	71	16	27	43	17	135
2006–07	Boston	80	11	32	43	–21	100

Chapter Seven

Eric Brewer

The New Breed

Most kids growing up playing hockey in Canada in the 1980s all wanted to be like Wayne Gretzky—to score goal upon goal and hear the crowd roar their name in celebration. Unless he is Bobby Orr, a defenseman is not likely to receive the same admiration from the public and is more prone to receive the crowd's anger when he makes a mistake, for as the hockey idiom states, "You never notice when a defenseman is doing a good job."

But destiny had a strange way of finding a young Eric Brewer. The coach put an unhappy Brewer on defense because the boy was the strongest back-skater on his atom team, and to this day, there he remains, seeing himself in no other position on the ice. "I wasn't crazy about it at first, but I was one of the strongest kids at skating backwards," said Brewer.

Encouraged to stick with the position, Brewer began to like being a defenseman and learned to appreciate the responsibility that comes with the territory. As he got older, his skating improved, as did his ability to read how a play would develop. Soon, people began to take notice, and the junior hockey scouts came knocking at the Brewer family home in Vernon, British Columbia.

Brewer could have opted for the U.S. college route with lucrative scholarship offers, but because he was just 16 years old, he and his family decided it was a better fit to have him play in the Western Hockey League. In the 1994 WHL bantam draft, Brewer was selected 81st overall by the Prince George Cougars, who played just a six-hour drive from home. Brewer settled in immediately in the new city, but it took a little longer for him to acclimatize himself to the play of the WHL. In his first year with the more skilled players, he struggled to keep up, scoring only 4 goals and 10 assists in 63 games, but in the next season, he more than doubled his point production to 5 goals and 25 assists in 71 games and was a major factor in his team's success in making it deep into the playoffs.

It was around this time that the pro scouts started to take notice of the six-foot-three-inch defenseman. With a unique vision of the ice and a great skating ability, Brewer was predicted to be the top defensive selection in the 1997 NHL entry draft, held in Pittsburgh. As predicted, the talented center from Sault Sainte Marie, Joe Thornton, went first overall in the draft, but Brewer did not have to wait long: he was quickly snapped up by the New York Islanders fifth overall. But he was still only 18 years old, and the Islanders wanted to keep him with the Prince George Cougars for one more season to make sure he was both physically and mentally ready to face the pressures of the National Hockey League.

The 1997–98 WHL season started off very well for Brewer. He surpassed his previous season's points totals in just 34 games, but his breakthrough season was cut short when he suffered a deep thigh bruise that kept him out for the remainder of the regular season. He returned in time for the Cougars' run in the playoffs, but they were eliminated in the second round.

During his time with the Cougars, Brewer improved his game significantly. He bettered his skating, he put on a few more pounds of muscle and his shot was good enough to beat the NHL's top goaltenders. In his first year with Prince George, he lacked confidence in his game, but with a little hard work, he became one of the team's best players when under pressure and a contributor in the dressing room. However, he still wasn't quite ready for the responsibilities and pressures of the big league.

The New York Islanders wanted to test the kid's skills at a professional level, and in the process did more damage than good. Under head coach Butch Goring, Brewer played 63 games, but he was used sparingly during those games and was benched on a regular basis, which never allowed the rookie a chance to learn from his mistakes. By the end of the 1998–99 season, he had only 5 goals, 6 assists and a plus/minus rating of –14. The next season, Brewer returned to the Islanders but again was grossly underused, playing in only 26 games with the Islanders and splitting his time with the American Hockey League's Lowell Lock Monsters.

With his confidence in the dumps, Brewer tried to prove himself to the New York Islanders coaching staff, but the team was floating near the bottom of the league and looking to rebuild around a group of young prospects. This meant that Brewer no longer fit in with the team's plan and was on the trading block during the summer of 2000. On June 24, 2000, Brewer was traded to the Edmonton Oilers in return for defenseman and one-time first-overall draft pick Roman

Hamrlik. Brewer was not exactly sad about his trade to the Oilers. It brought him closer to his family and to a fan base that was a lot more passionate about the game of hockey than its Islander counterparts. "I think the trade just gave me a chance to reflect and realize that things are never as bad as you might think, that you just can't be too hard on yourself," said Brewer.

With the Oilers, Brewer finally blossomed into the player the Islanders had wanted when they selected him fifth overall in 1997. Oilers assistant coach and former defensive defenseman Charlie Huddy took Brewer under his wing and worked on the small aspects of his game. Brewer had the basics; he just needed some minor refinements to become a top NHL defenseman. In his first few games as an Oiler, Brewer showed that he had finally realized his potential. The Oilers' focus on good hockey rather than the business of the game proved the perfect breeding ground for Brewer's talent. In his first season with the Edmonton Oilers, he scored 7 goals and 14 assists and added a plus/minus rating of +15 to his stats. Brewer's first taste of the post-season, however, would not be as successful as his regular season. The Dallas Stars eliminated the Oilers in an exciting six-game series. Brushing off the early exit from the playoffs, Brewer returned to the Oilers lineup with a mission to prove himself and contribute to the Oilers as much as possible in a successful season.

The season started off normally, and Brewer was showing gradual improvement with every game, but never in his life did he expect to get a call from the director of the Canadian men's national hockey team asking him to be part of Canada's bid for gold in the 2002 Winter Olympics in Salt Lake City. Brewer was not new to international hockey, having played in the World Junior Championship in 1998 and with Team Canada for the World Championship in 2001, but this was the Olympics, and Brewer felt that there were other more experienced players who could take his place. When selecting the team, executive director Wayne Gretzky felt that Brewer's size, defensive skills and youthful enthusiasm would bring to the team an element that a veteran defenseman could not provide. Brewer passed the difficult Olympic training program and earned himself a spot on the team beside the best Canadian players in the game. "When I found out I was on the Olympic team, it was like: Wow, this is probably the best team in the world. This is it!" said Brewer in Jeff Rudd's book, *Hockey's Young Superstars*.

Brewer was not far off in his estimation of the team being the best in the world, because just a couple of weeks later, Team Canada won a gold medal victory over Team USA. Brewer helped the cause with 2 goals of his own in one of the proudest moments of his as-yet-short career. When Brewer returned to the Oilers, he came back with more than just a gold medal; he now had the confidence that anything could be achieved with a little hard work. The Oilers, unfortunately, could not share in that same enthusiasm, and they missed out on the 2002 playoffs by only a couple of points.

The next season, despite his 8 goals and 21 assists, Brewer was heavily criticized for the worst plus/minus rating on the team, at –11. But considering he was logging over 25 minutes per game, it is hard to criticize him for the statistical shortcoming. The Oilers managed to sneak into the 2003 playoffs that year, only to meet up against hated playoff rivals the Dallas Stars, and, once again, the Oilers bowed out early in six games despite Brewer's 4 points and plus/minus rating of +1.

Brewer was adapting nicely to his environment in Edmonton, and the fans were beginning to appreciate him. The 2003–04 season was another successful one for Brewer, and in 77 games played, he recorded 25 points. But the Oilers failed to make the playoffs again, and

Brewer found himself waiting for over another year as the NHL and its Players' Association sorted out their differences so hockey could return for the 2005–06 season. Before Brewer ever got to start training for the upcoming season, however, the Oilers decided that they wanted a veteran defenseman on their blue line. Brewer, along with teammates Doug Lynch and Jeff Woywitka, was traded to St. Louis in return for the Blues captain, Chris Pronger.

Following the same patterns through much of his career, Brewer's first year with the Blues was unlucky: his season was cut short at just 32 games after he dislocated his left shoulder. Brewer returned for the 2006–07 season ready for the challenge of another year and helped his sparsely talented team to a decent record of 32 wins, 34 losses and 13 overtime losses. One day, when the stars align for Brewer, he will find himself on a Stanley Cup–contending team and will get to hold that coveted piece of silver over his head for the first time in his professional career. With his talent, not many who have followed his career thus far doubt that it can happen.

Season	Team	GP	Goals	Assists	Points	+/-	Penalties
1998–99	NY Islanders	63	5	6	11	–14	32
1999–2000	NY Islanders	26	0	2	2	–11	20
2000–01	Edmonton	77	7	14	21	15	53
2001–02	Edmonton	81	7	18	25	–5	45
2002–03	Edmonton	80	8	21	29	–11	45
2003–04	Edmonton	77	7	18	25	–6	67
2005–06	St. Louis	32	6	3	9	–17	45
2006–07	St. Louis	82	11	23	29	–10	69

Chapter Eight

Chris Pronger

The Not-So-Gentle Giant

There are a select few players who are destined from an early age to play in the National Hockey League, but everyone who saw him play knew that Chris Pronger had every quality that any team would want on their side.

Born in 1974 in the hockey-addicted town of Dryden, Ontario, Chris Pronger was immediately enthralled with the game of hockey. Chris and his older brother, Sean, cut their playing teeth in the minor system in Dryden but quickly moved beyond those boundaries as they grew older. Sean was the first to get noticed and joined the Bowling Green State University (NCAA) in Ohio, wanting a backup plan if his hockey career did not lead him to the NHL. Chris wanted to follow in his brother's footsteps, but he was drafted from the Stratford Cullitons Junior B of the Ontario Hockey Association to the Peterborough Petes of the Ontario Hockey League. The Petes was the perfect training ground for the young Pronger; countless NHL players, including Steve Yzerman, Larry Murphy and Bob Gainey, came out of the Petes system and went on to stellar professional careers.

At six feet, six inches tall, Pronger was a valuable asset to the Petes' defensive core, but for such a large player, he proved equally adept on the attack and was a regular contributor on the power plays, often pinching in from the line to score goals. In his first season with the Petes, Pronger tallied a respectable 17 goals and 45 assists, for 62 points, placing fifth in scoring on the team during the 1991–92 season. The following season, Pronger improved further, racking up 15 goals and 62 assists, for 77 points. But it wasn't just his ability on the offense that had NHL teams salivating to get their hands on him during the 1993 NHL entry draft; Pronger was an all-round triple threat. He could get the points, put up a wall on the blue line and use his rather large frame to pound his opponents into submission along the boards—all qualities that teams would love to add to their blue lines, especially packaged in one player.

The 1993 draft was rife with talent, but it was a guarantee that Pronger would be selected among the top five players. Any team lucky enough to get one of the top five selections had a difficult decision to make with players like Paul Kariya, Rob Niedermayer and Alexandre Daigle up for grabs. But players of Pronger's size and skill on the blue line are hard to come by, so it was no surprise when Pronger was chosen second overall by the Hartford Whalers, behind the eventually disappointing number one pick, Alexandre Daigle.

The Whalers were in desperate need of some young talent on the blue line, having finished the 1992–93 season with 369 goals against, compared to the 230 goals let in by the best team that year, the Chicago Blackhawks. Pronger received a baptism by fire in his first season, playing in 81 of 84 games. But the addition of Pronger on defense could do little to fill the holes on the team. The Whalers ended up with the third-worst record in the 1993–94 season, with 63 points and not much hope for the next year. The lockout-shortened 1994–95 season did nothing to help the Whalers or Pronger, and the team once again finished out of the playoffs. In 43 regular-season games, Pronger had just 5 goals and 9 assists, but more telling was his plus/minus rating of –12.

As bad as things were going on the ice, Pronger's personal problems began to leak into the media. He was often cited in the newspapers as immature and unable to handle the pressure of the NHL. Pronger showed his immaturity off the ice by getting into a well-publicized barroom brawl and was even arrested for a drunk-driving offense.

His antics on and off the ice did not earn him any supporters in the Whalers front office, so during the off-season, it was decided that the team needed someone who could focus on the game and put the puck in the net. In a one-for-one deal, Pronger was traded to the St. Louis Blues for star forward Brendan Shanahan, a deal that on paper seemed to work in favor of the Whalers rather than the Blues. The people of St. Louis felt the same way and did not exactly welcome young Pronger with open arms. Shanahan went on to score 44 goals in the 1995–96 season, while Pronger struggled to find his pre-NHL ways with just 7 goals and 18 assists in 78 games.

Coming into the St. Louis market, it seemed Pronger was unaware of the love the city had for Shanahan. "Hartford isn't exactly a media hotbed either, so you don't really get the correlation of the two cities and you don't get to read about other players, whether it be from St. Louis or other areas," said Pronger in a 2000 interview with NHL.com. "So I didn't realize the type of respect and the type of player Brendan had become here in St. Louis. You know he scored 50 goals and all those things, but you don't realize what a pillar of the community he was and the things that he did off the ice that everybody loved him for."

Despite the challenges, under the iron fists of head coach Mike Keenan, Pronger was forced to follow the coach's system, and slowly he began to regain the form that saw him drafted second overall. He went from a –18 rating in his first season with the Blues to a +15 rating in 1996–97 season. In addition to improving his stats, Pronger was becoming the physically dominating player that he was in his junior days, and he was earning the respect of the St. Louis fans.

When Keenan left the Blues organization during the 1996–97 season, he was replaced with the more soft-handed Joel Quenneville, and Pronger developed into the player the Blues had hoped for when they parted with Shanahan, who was traded to the Detroit Red Wings just one season after the Whalers had acquired him. "Joel was the perfect coach for me," said Pronger in a 2006 interview with NHL.com. "As a former NHL defenseman, he, too, knew how to pick out the things I needed to improve on and how to get me to that point."

Pronger came into his own as one of the premier defensemen in the league during the 1997–98 season. No longer was he getting caught out of position or turning over the puck; he was now the coach's number one defenseman in pressure situations, sometimes logging up to 25 minutes of ice time per game. Quenneville had such faith the in young defenseman's new-found confidence that he named him the team captain at the start of the season, replacing Wayne Gretzky, who had been traded to the New York Rangers. Alongside Pronger, the Blues started to turn their fortunes around and finished the season with 98 points, their highest point total since the 1990–91 season, when they reached 105 points.

Pronger helped the Blues defeat the Los Angeles Kings in the first round of the playoffs with an easy four-game sweep, but it was the series against the Detroit Red Wings that would change everything for him. After five grueling games, it looked inevitable that the Red Wings would pull off the win, but Pronger knew that it would take only a little hard work for the team to fight back. That attitude put him in the line of fire of a Red Wings point shot that hit him squarely in the chest over his heart and sent his six-foot-six-inch frame crashing to the ice. Players from both sides waved frantically for the paramedics as they stood above Pronger's motionless body. A heart monitor showed that although his heart had not stopped completely, it was skipping at an irregular rate. The players and medical staff breathed a collective sigh of relief when he began to move his arms and legs. Pronger was carried off on a stretcher and taken directly to the hospital.

"There was no blinding light, no angels coming to take me home," Pronger told NHL.com. "Everyone tells me how concerned they were for me, but I don't remember much of that. When I woke up, I thought about Mother's Day and then, when I saw Al MacInnis standing over me, praying, all I could remember were those many stories Al tells me about lobster traps and how he unloaded them for pocket change on the docks in Nova Scotia when he was growing up."

By now, Pronger had earned the respect of his coach and teammates with his solid play on the ice, and he had racked up the best plus/minus rating in the league with a +47, good enough to take home the prestigious Bud Light Trophy. After another good year with the Blues in the 1998–99 season, Pronger was now leaps and bounds away from the lanky, immature, self-destructive rookie that broke into the league in 1993. His name was being mentioned in the same breath as other legendary greats such as Larry Robinson and fellow contemporaries such as Rob

Blake and Al MacInnis. Pronger proved his talents with a career year during the 1999–2000 season, scoring 14 goals and 48 assists.

The St. Louis Blues, a team that nobody had ever given any credit, finished the season with the most points in the league for the first time since joining the NHL in the 1967 expansion, taking home the President's Trophy for their efforts. The team had a veteran and leader in their captain, Chris Pronger, solid goaltending from Roman Turek and reliable scoring from a host of players, including Pavol Demitra and Pierre Turgeon—all elements that would make them good contenders for the Stanley Cup. After such a remarkable personal and team year, this was Pronger's best hope to date at making it to the finals. Unfortunately for the Blues, they came up againts the San Jose Sharks in the first round. Whether the Blues underestimated them or the Sharks had a greater desire to win, the Blues had to fight just to get the series into the seventh game, in which they were eliminated in a 3–1 loss on home ice.

It was a hard loss for Pronger to take after having worked so hard to get to the top of the league, but when the individual awards were being given out at the end of the year, he did receive a small consolation prize. Pronger became the first defenseman to win both the Norris Trophy as the league's best defenseman and the Hart Trophy as the league's most valuable player since Bobby Orr did it in 1972. Pronger also added another Bud Light Trophy to his collection, with a league-leading plus/minus rating of +52.

For the next couple of years, the St. Louis Blues continued to entertain fans during the regular season, but the post-season proved disappointing. In 2001, the Blues were eliminated in the conference finals by the Colorado Avalanche, and in 2002, by the eventual champions, the Detroit Red Wings, in the conference semi-finals. However, 2002 was not a complete let-down: Pronger helped the Canadian national hockey team to its first Olympic gold medal in 50 years. He would have liked to add the Stanley Cup to the gold medal, but not everyone can have it all.

After an injury-plagued season in 2002–03 that saw him play only five games, Pronger bounced back during the 2003–04 season, potting 14 goals and 40 assists, but, yet again, the Blues were eliminated in the first round of the playoffs. Following the 2004–05 lockout and the salary cap imposed on teams, the St. Louis Blues found they could no longer afford the hefty salary a player of Pronger's caliber commanded, so the beloved Blues captain became an Edmonton Oiler for the start of the 2005–06 season.

With Pronger quarterbacking their defense, the Edmonton Oilers were able to make a push for the final playoff spot in their division, with hope for a shot at the Stanley Cup. No one gave the Oilers any chance of making it deep into the playoffs, but as if by some predestined miracle, the perfect blend of young talent and veteran know-how got the Oilers into the Stanley Cup finals against the Carolina Hurricanes. Pronger was one of the major reasons the Oilers found themselves in this position. With his excellent vision of the ice surface, Pronger often started the plays that led to Oilers goals, and his positioning on the ice made it difficult for the opposition to get anywhere near Oilers goaltender Dwayne Roloson. It was exactly this leadership and skill that the Oilers relied upon after their number one goaltender went down with an injury in the first game of the finals and had to be replaced by the backup goaltender for the remainder of the series. It was also in the first game of the series that Pronger became the first player in the history of the National Hockey League to score on a penalty shot in the Stanley Cup finals. But despite his team-leading 5 goals and 16 assists in the playoffs, the Oilers could not hold on to the series and lost to the Hurricanes in seven games.

Shortly after suffering the heartbreaking loss of another Stanley Cup in Edmonton, Oilers fans received another blow in June 2006, when Pronger suddenly requested a trade, citing personal reasons. Although never confirmed by Pronger himself, it was widely reported by the media that Pronger's wife was unhappy in Edmonton. He was traded to the Anaheim Ducks in return for Joffrey Lupul, Ladislav Smid and several draft picks. While Edmonton fans boo him mercilessly every time he plays his old team, the Anaheim Ducks are happy they got their hands on a possible future Hall of Fame defenseman.

The 2007 Stanley Cup playoffs proved to be Pronger's year. The Ducks used their superior defense and excellent goaltending to make it all the way to the finals against the Ottawa Senators. Pronger was the focus of controversy during the playoffs, after receiving a one-game suspension for a hit from behind on the Detroit Red Wings' Tomas Holmstrom in the conference finals. Pronger felt he did not deserve the suspension and publicly blamed the Canadian sports media for pressuring the league to suspend him. Controversy again followed Pronger into the Stanley Cup finals, when he delivered a elbow to the head of Senators captain Daniel Alfredsson. Pronger received another one-game suspension. Despite the two suspensions, Pronger was a major factor in the Ducks' success, playing up to 30 minutes per game and scoring 3 goals and 12 assists. The Ducks put the Senators out of their misery in five games, and Pronger finally had the Stanley Cup he had dreamed of all his life.

Season	Team	GP	Goals	Assists	Points	+/-	Penalties
1993–94	Hartford	81	5	25	30	–3	113
1994–95	Hartford	43	5	9	14	–12	54
1995–96	St. Louis	78	7	18	25	–18	110
1996–97	St. Louis	79	11	24	35	15	143
1997–98	St. Louis	81	9	27	36	47	180
1998–99	St. Louis	67	13	33	46	3	113
1999–2000	St. Louis	79	14	48	62	52	92
2000–01	St. Louis	51	8	39	47	23	120
2001–02	St. Louis	78	7	40	47	23	120
2002–03	St. Louis	5	1	3	4	–2	10
2003–04	St. Louis	80	14	40	54	–1	88
2005–06	Edmonton	80	12	44	56	2	74
2006–07	Anaheim	66	13	46	59	27	69

Chapter Nine

Chris Chelios
The Ageless Wonder

Although there were rumors that the 2006–07 season would be Chris Chelios' final one, he re-signed with the Detroit Red Wings for another year. Now going into his 24th season in the NHL, Chelios has been a force in the league ever since he started as a rookie with the Montréal Canadiens in 1983.

Born Christos Kostas Tselios on January 25, 1962, in Chicago, Illinois, Chris Chelios, as he is more commonly known, took to hockey at an early age. Growing up in Chicago in the late 1960s and early 1970s, a young Chelios had a long list of NHL players he idolized. The Blackhawks had legends such as Stan Mikita, Bobby Hull and Tony Esposito, and he could not help but marvel at the Hawks' rival's best player, the Bruins' Bobby Orr. However, as much as he enjoyed hockey, Chelios was a die-hard fan of the Chicago Bears, especially the tough linebacker

Dick Butkus, and still to this day, Chelios cheers for the Chicago Bears.

But it was on the ice that Chelios found he fit in the most. He played with various teams around his Chicago neighborhood, and when his parents packed up and moved to the San Diego area in 1977, the warm weather and beautiful beaches did not deter him from pursuing his dream of making it into the National Hockey League. He soon found himself back in the cold north, playing with the Moose Jaw Canucks of the Saskatchewan Junior Hockey League before moving back to the United States to play for the University of Wisconsin Badgers. It was during his days with the Badgers that the Montréal Canadiens took notice of the fast young defenseman. While some defensemen are focused purely on the defense of their territory and others add a more offensive component to the game, Chelios was equally adept in both roles. The Montréal Canadiens wanted a good two-way defenseman, so they snatched him up in the 1981 NHL entry draft in the second round, 40th overall.

Chelios spent two more years in Wisconsin before receiving the call to join the Canadiens for a few games during the 1983–84 NHL season. In the 12 games he played, Chelios impressed the Canadiens coaches enough to earn a regular spot on the team in the playoffs against first-round opponents the Boston Bruins. Chelios helped the Canadiens sweep past the Bruins and dispense of the Québec Nordiques in a very physical six-game series. He would not get the dream rookie season he wanted because the defending champions, the New York Islanders, eliminated the Canadiens in the conference finals. But in the 15 games he played in the playoffs, Chelios scored 1 goal and 9 assists and played with a maturity and drive that made it easy to decide to make him a permanent fixture on the Montréal blue line.

Chelios was a good player in his first few years, earning 64 points in his first full year with the Canadiens in 1984–85 and helping a young group of Canadiens to a Stanley Cup in 1986. The 1985–86 Canadiens were not exactly Cup contenders, going into the playoffs with a team stacked with rookies; however, it was exactly those rookie players who brought the energy the team needed to get them far into the playoffs. They swept past the Boston Bruins in the first round, escaped by the skin of their teeth in overtime of the seventh game in the second round against the Hartford Whalers and took out the New York Rangers in five games in the conference finals, making it into the finals for the first time since they last held the Cup in 1979. Chelios was a solid contributor throughout the playoffs, keeping his game more on the defensive side to allow for the occasional mistake made by the rookie-laden team. The Canadiens had momentum going into the finals against the Calgary Flames and finished them off in five games. Chelios finished the playoffs with 2 goals and 9 assists, and in just three seasons in the National Hockey League, he had a Stanley Cup.

With each passing season, Chelios got better and better, earning himself a special reputation in the league. It was during the 1988–89 season that Chelios became one of the premier defensemen in the league. He finished the season with an impressive 73 points in 80 games and a plus/minus rating of +35. He added to that list his selection to the first All-Star team and earned the Norris Trophy as the league's best defenseman, over other favorites such as Al MacInnis and Ray Bourque. Aside from the excellent stats and all the accolades, Chelios contributed to his team in a way that is sometimes just as important as points—he was the best at getting under the skin of his opponents.

After coming in second in points at the end of the regular season, the Montréal Canadiens were one of the favorites going into the playoffs, riding high on the success of their strong defense and the excellent goaltending from Patrick Roy.

The strong regular season continued into the playoffs, where Montréal easily shook off the Hartford Whalers and the Boston Bruins before coming up against the Philadelphia Flyers in the conference finals. It was in this series against the Flyers that Chelios showed his true fighting spirit. Early in the series, he delivered a violent check to Flyers forward Brian Propp. The impact left Propp with a concussion, forcing him to miss one game. The Flyers and their fans made it their mission to make the rest of the series a living hell for Chelios, giving him their unwanted attention every time he touched the puck. But like a true champion, Chelios was completely unfazed, much to the frustration of temperamental Flyers goaltender Ron Hextall. In game six of the series, when it was apparent that the Canadiens were going to eliminate the Flyers, Hextall took it upon himself to seek revenge on Chelios for his hit on Propp. As soon as Chelios crossed into the Flyers zone with the puck, Hextall bolted directly at him, swung his goalie stick at Chelios and tackled him to the ice, while repeatedly raining blows on his head with his blocker. Hextall was ejected from the game, and the Canadiens went on to the Stanley Cup finals, but lost to the Calgary Flames in six games.

The next season with the Canadiens, Chelios was named co-captain with Guy Carbonneau, but his time as captain in Montréal was short-lived. He was traded midway through the season to the Chicago Blackhawks in return for Denis Savard. Chicago wanted to add a skilled veteran presence to their blue line to back up their young goaltending prospect, Ed Belfour. Chelios fit in well in his native Chicago, and the Blackhawks suddenly became one of the more dominant teams in the league, so much so that they finished the 1990–91 season first overall with 106 points. But as seasoned hockey fans know, the playoffs are a different season altogether, and the Blackhawks learned that lesson in the first round, when the Minnesota North Stars, who finished the regular season with 68 points, eliminated Chelios' team in six games.

Now at the peak of his career, Chelios pushed as hard as he could to help his native Chicago back to Stanley Cup contention because the city had been starving for a hockey championship since 1961. But the hockey gods can be cruel, as the older Chicago fans knew all too well. Chelios put in another season worthy of a Norris nomination, and though the Blackhawks fell short of their previous season's successes, they still had a position in the playoffs. Surprising the critics who said the Hawks were riding the success of their goaltender, Chicago made it past the St. Louis Blues in six games, dispensed with the Detroit Red Wings in four straight, and beat up on the Edmonton Oilers in the conference finals to make it to the bright lights of the Stanley Cup finals against the defending champs, the Pittsburgh Penguins. In the end, the firepower of the Penguins, with players such as Mario Lemieux, Kevin Stevens and a young Jaromir Jagr, was just too much for Chelios and the Hawks, and they went down in four straight games.

Chelios met his career-high season total in 1992–93 with another 73 points overall, and for his efforts on the Chicago blue line, he took home another Norris Trophy. But Chelios had to watch most of the playoffs from home after Chicago was eliminated in the first round by the St. Louis Blues, while his former team, the Montréal Canadiens, went on to win the Stanley Cup.

Another few seasons passed, and though the Blackhawks continued to play well in the regular season, they never seemed to have Lady Luck on their side when it came time for the playoffs. In 1994, they were eliminated in the first round by the Toronto Maple Leafs; in 1995, they were eliminated in the third round by the Detroit Red Wings; in 1996, they were eliminated in the second round by the Colorado Avalanche; in 1997, they were eliminated in the first round by the

Colorado Avalanche; and in 1998, they missed the playoffs altogether.

On an individual level, however, Chelios continued to thrive. He was given the captaincy of the Blackhawks at the beginning of the 1995–96 season, and he won his third Norris Trophy at the end of the season after another all-around stellar performance. But after over a decade in the National Hockey League defending against some of the biggest and toughest players in the world, age looked like it had finally started to catch up with the veteran defenseman. His point totals started to drop, and though his defensive skills never waned, the Blackhawks needed a player who could contribute on the offense. By the 1998–99 season, the Blackhawks' offensive production had fallen to the bottom of the league, and it became clear to Chelios that management was going to have to rebuild around some younger players. At 37 years of age, Chelios was definitely past his prime, but he felt that he still had something to contribute. Plenty of teams were interested in Chelios, but he wanted to be part of a high-scoring team that would not need him to score the game-winning goals, but draw from his wealth of experience on the ice and in the dressing room. That team turned out to be the Detroit Red Wings.

Detroit was the perfect fit for Chelios. With a good group of veterans and dynamic young talent, he felt that they could make a proper charge in the playoffs and avoid the curse that continually befell the Blackhawks. In his second season with the Wings, Chelios succumbed to injuries and played in only 24 games, but when he returned for the 2001–02 season, he played in 79 full games and recorded a respectable 6 goals, 33 assists and a plus/minus rating of +40. Halfway through the season, he also participated in the Winter Olympics in Salt Lake City, helping the U.S. national men's hockey team to a silver medal and receiving a mention to the tournament's All-Star team.

Back in Detroit, while defensive partner Nicklas Lidstrom took home the Norris Trophy as top blue liner, Chelios quietly walked away with the Bud Light Trophy for the best plus/minus rating. His team didn't do that badly either, finishing in the top spot at the end of the regular season and going all the way in the playoffs to win the Stanley Cup. It was his second Stanley Cup, and the 40-year-old cherished every moment.

Those who thought Chelios would take this high moment in his career to bow out of hockey and enjoy his retirement before an injury ended it for him really do not know Chris Chelios.

Although he doesn't score like he used to, he remains a solid presence on the Detroit blue line.

Season	Team	GP	Goals	Assists	Points	+/-	Penalties
1983–84	Montréal	12	0	2	2	–5	12
1984–85	Montréal	74	9	55	64	11	87
1985–86	Montréal	41	8	26	34	4	67
1986–87	Montréal	71	11	33	44	–5	124
1987–88	Montréal	71	20	41	61	14	172
1988–89	Montréal	80	15	58	73	35	185
1989–90	Montréal	53	9	22	31	20	136
1990–91	Chicago	77	12	52	64	23	192
1991–92	Chicago	80	9	47	56	24	245
1992–93	Chicago	84	15	58	73	14	282
1993–94	Chicago	76	16	44	60	12	212
1994–95	Chicago	48	5	33	38	17	72
1995–96	Chicago	81	14	58	72	25	140
1996–97	Chicago	72	10	38	48	16	112
1997–98	Chicago	81	3	39	42	–7	151
1998–99	Chicago	65	8	26	34	–4	89
1998–99	Detroit	10	1	1	2	5	4
1999–2000	Detroit	81	3	31	34	48	103
2000–01	Detroit	24	0	3	3	4	45
2001–02	Detroit	79	6	33	39	40	126
2002–03	Detroit	66	2	17	19	4	78
2003–04	Detroit	69	2	19	21	12	61
2005–06	Detroit	81	4	7	11	22	108
2006–07	Detroit	71	0	11	11	11	34

Chapter Ten

Nicklas Lidstrom

Simply the Best!

Nicklas Lidstrom has been an integral part of the Detroit Red Wings blue line since he first broke into the league in 1991. In Lidstrom's rookie season, head coach Bryan Murray had enough confidence in the young Swedish defensive prodigy to play him in all 80 games, and since that year, Lidstrom has firmly held his position on the Detroit blue line.

Lidstrom grew up in Vasteras, Sweden, and while most young players his age wanted to play forward and score all the goals, he did not mind playing defense. For Lidstrom, hockey has never been about personal glory, and as a defenseman, he is able to contribute to both offensive and defensive parts of the game. Coaches of the young Lidstrom recognized his early maturity and knew that he would soon make his way into the professional ranks. His work ethic was apparent from early on, and it finally paid off when he got his first professional gig with his hometown club, Vasteras IK, of the Swedish Elitserien.

Lidstrom had limited ice time in his rookie season with the team, playing in just 20 games; however, the Detroit Red Wings' scouts knew that Lidstrom had the basic skills that would enable him to develop into a top defenseman. Just before the start of his second season with Vasteras IK, Lidstrom was drafted 53rd overall by the Detroit Red Wings, who used their third overall pick to secure the young, stable defenseman. The Red Wings were desperate for some good young talent in their organization after decades of being at the bottom of league. They needed a defensive defenseman, but Lidstrom still needed a couple more years of development before joining the best players in the National Hockey League.

In his next two years with Vasteras IK, Lidstrom improved his point production and defensive skills to such a degree that the Detroit Red Wings felt comfortable enough to add him to their regular lineup. He had performed beyond expectations in training camp and the pre-season exhibition games to earn the coaches' confidence, something that is difficult for a rookie to accomplish. The Detroit coaching staff recognized his work ethic and rewarded him with a spot on the team. Lidstrom brought a much-needed reliability to the blue line that helped turn the middle-of-the-pack team into a Stanley Cup contender.

Lidstrom may not have been solely responsible for the turnaround in the Red Wings' game, considering they had Steve Yzerman and a young, speedy Russian named Sergei Fedorov. But in terms of defense, Detroit had allowed 298 goals against in the 1990–91 season before the arrival of Lidstrom, and with Lidstrom on the team for the 1991–92 season, the team decreased their goals-against total to 256. This change occurred with the same goaltender (Tim Cheveldae) and the same coaching staff, so Lidstrom's arrival was an obvious boost to the struggling Detroit defense. Those in charge of selecting players for the awards given out at the end of the year were in agreement about Lidstrom's contribution to the team (11 goals, 49 assists, 60 points), naming him as one of the nominees in the running for the Calder Trophy as the Rookie of the Year. Unfortunately, a young Russian forward named Pavel Bure stole the spotlight and took home the trophy—flashy goal-scoring always seems to win out over solid defense. But the snub did not bother Lidstrom because he had his sights set on a bigger piece of silverware.

From 1991 to 1994, Lidstrom was a consistent presence on the Detroit blue line, playing in every game over the three seasons and thriving with a maximum amount of ice time. But with the NHL players' strike at the beginning of the 1994–95 season, Lidstrom was not content to sit on his couch at home and wait for the two sides to come to an agreement, so he packed his gear and returned to his hometown to play 13 games for his old team, Vasteras IK. When the NHL season returned in January 1995, Lidstrom resumed his spot on the Detroit blue line and helped lead the team to first place overall, a spot they had not occupied since the 1964–65 season, back when the league consisted of only six teams.

The 1995 Stanley Cup playoffs were looking good for the Red Wings. They beat the Dallas Stars in the first round in five games, bowled over the San Jose Sharks in the second round in four straight and put away the Chicago Blackhawks in a close series in which three games were decided in overtime, with Detroit coming out on the winning end in five games. This was the first time since the 1966 Stanley Cup finals that the Red Wings had made it to the big show. (They lost the 1966 finals to the Montréal Canadiens.) Despite Lidstrom's 4 goals and 12 assists, the Red Wings couldn't manage a win against the New Jersey Devils and their young upstart goaltender, Martin

Brodeur. The Devils won their franchise's first-ever Stanley Cup, while the Red Wings would have to wait a couple of years before they would get another chance at the big prize.

The 1995–96 season saw the Detroit Red Wings set a new NHL team record with 62 wins during the regular season, and Lidstrom achieved a career high of 17 goals and 50 assists, for 67 points. The numbers obviously made the Red Wings the favorites to win the Cup, but the playoffs run by a different set of rules, and anything can happen. Detroit made it past the Winnipeg Jets and the St. Louis Blues, but conference rivals the Colorado Avalanche put a stop to the Wings' season in the conference finals in an entertaining six-game series. All seemed set for the Red Wings to finally break their long-standing, 41-year Stanley Cup drought, but it all came apart. Yet with Scotty Bowman as their coach—the coach with the most career victories—few people counted the Wings out from returning to form for the 1996–97 season.

It is difficult to find a peak in Lidstrom's career because he has been remarkably consistent since breaking into the league, but during the late 1990s, he was well on his way to becoming a mature player. While other defensemen at the time such as Scott Stevens and Al MacInnis relied on their hard checking and blistering slap shots, Lidstrom was the kind of defenseman that most spectators don't notice when he is on the ice. And it is just that kind of defenseman that every team needs to be successful. Lidstrom exhibited a kind of quiet control when he was on the ice, preferring to rely on his unique ability to read the development of the play rather than bash an opponent into oblivion like Scott Stevens would. Lidstrom's preference was to use brain over brawn, using his quick skating ability to move himself into position to intercept the puck or the player and cause turnovers. Although he always ranked as one of the higher-scoring defensemen, never shying away from pinching in on the offense, Lidstrom never neglected his duties on the blue line, never finishing a season with a plus/minus rating below +7.

Lidstrom and the Red Wings lived up to their hype and made it back into the playoffs in 1997 for a first-round match-up against the St. Louis Blues. Lidstrom was his regular solid self during the entire series, not contributing much on the offense but holding the Wings' blue line and frustrating the Blues at every turn. The same pattern continued in the second round against the Anaheim Mighty Ducks, with the Red Wings defeating them in four straight games. Detroit then met the Colorado Avalanche in a rematch of the 1996 conference finals series. It was a close and contentious match, but the Red Wings came out on top, and Lidstrom had himself another chance at the Stanley Cup against the Philadelphia Flyers. This time around, the Red Wings were the far superior team and easily ran over the Flyers in four straight games. Lidstrom was finally able to raise the Stanley Cup above his head.

Lidstrom never missed a beat during the 1997–98 season, logging the most ice time for a defenseman and still recording all-star statistics. He matched his career high of 17 goals and kept his defensive stats up to par with a plus/minus rating of +22. As Lidstrom's season went, so did the Red Wings'. The team finished once again among the top teams in the league. Lidstrom stepped up his offensive contribution in the 1998 playoffs as the Red Wings made their way through the Phoenix Coyotes, St. Louis Blues and Dallas Stars to return to the Stanley Cup finals and face the Washington Capitals. The Wings once again swept their way to the Cup, with all players contributing to a dominating performance. Lidstrom had his best playoff points performance, potting 6 goals and assisting his teammates 13 times, for 19 points.

Although the Wings did not make it back to the Stanley Cup during the next three seasons,

Lidstrom's star continued to rise. The NHL finally recognized his commitment to his teammates and his job on defense when he was awarded the Norris Trophy as the top defenseman for the 2000–01 season. As proud as he was of his personal achievements, things would only get better for the Swedish defenseman in the 2001–02 season.

The veteran-laden Red Wings returned to the top of the league with 116 points to take home the President's Trophy. Lidstrom had another great defensive year, quietly doing his job on the blue line, keeping his team in every game. As Lidstrom turned from a rookie to a veteran, his points steadily increased, along with his ice time. On a good night, it was not uncommon for him to log 25 to 30 minutes of ice time and never once show signs of fatigue.

Going into the playoffs, the Red Wings were the obvious favorite, but being the favorite never guarantees a trip to the finals. Lidstrom knew his team had a good chance at making it all the way. But now, as a veteran of two Stanley Cup–winning teams, he knew that he could take nothing for granted, having also been to the finals and lost, and that he would probably have to work harder than ever. Fortunately, the hockey gods were on his side for the 2002 playoffs, and his

Red Wings cruised passed the Vancouver Canucks and the St. Louis Blues. They had a difficult conference final against hated rivals the Colorado Avalanche in a series that needed a full seven games to be decided, but they once again found themselves in the Cup finals, this time against the Carolina Hurricanes.

Carolina was able to put up a fight, but with veteran talent such as Steve Yzerman, Chris Chelios, Steve Duchesne, Dominik Hasek and, of course, Nicklas Lidstrom, the Red Wings were able to band together and finish the Hurricanes off in five games. For his consistent effort and reliable defense, Lidstrom was awarded the Conn Smythe Trophy as the Most Valuable Player in the playoffs. There were other players on the team who merited the award, such as Brett Hull, with 10 playoff goals, or goaltender Dominik Hasek, with a 1.86-goals-against average, but it was Lidstrom's 28 to 30 minutes of ice time and amazing defensive skills that won the day.

What made the trophy all the more sweet was that Lidstrom was the first-ever European player to win the award. "I was really surprised to win it," he said on the ice during the post-game celebration. "I wasn't even thinking about it, really. I'm more happy about winning another Cup, but winning the Conn Smythe is really an honor that I'll never forget."

It was his quiet commitment to the team and meticulous dedication to the details of his job that earned him the honor, and coach Scotty Bowman was not surprised to see him take home the Conn Smythe. "You look at what Nicklas Lidstrom did all the way through the playoffs, and he was just about a perfect player on the ice," said Bowman, who announced his retirement after the game. "It's really a wonderful tribute to him."

The accolades did not stop with the Stanley Cup and the Conn Smythe Trophy. For the second year in a row, Lidstrom earned top honors as the best defenseman, taking home another Norris Trophy. After another stellar season in 2002–03, Lidstrom again was named the league's top defenseman for his quiet commitment to the position. Scott Niedermayer broke Lidstrom's streak in the 2003–04 season, but after an 80-point season in 2005–06, Lidstrom again beat out the competition and walked away with another Norris Trophy for his collection. For the 2006–07 season, Lidstrom remained at the top of the defensemen in the league and again was the Norris Trophy champ, becoming the first five-time winner since Ray Bourque.

Lidstrom secured himself a spot in the history of the Detroit Red Wings when, before the start of the 2006–07 season, he was named team captain after the retirement of long-serving captain Steve Yzerman. Replacing Yzerman was not the easiest thing for a player to do, but there wasn't single player on the team more respected and liked than Lidstrom. It seemed like a natural evolution in his career to be given the honorable title.

Lidstrom is proof for all the younger defensemen in the league that if you have a strong commitment to working hard and playing the game with your head, success will come naturally. Playing essentially mistake-free hockey doesn't hurt his cause either. "He doesn't play a game that draws a lot of attention to himself. But if you know the game of hockey, you just see that he never makes a mistake," said former teammate Brendan Shanahan. "I can count on one hand the amount of mistakes Nicklas Lidstrom has made in the six years I've been with him. He's unbelievable."

Season	Team	GP	Goals	Assists	Points	+/-	Penalties
1991–92	Detroit	80	11	49	60	36	22
1992–93	Detroit	84	7	34	41	7	28
1993–94	Detroit	84	10	46	56	43	26
1994–95	Detroit	43	10	16	26	15	6
1995–96	Detroit	81	17	50	67	29	20
1996–97	Detroit	79	15	42	57	11	30
1997–98	Detroit	80	17	42	59	22	18
1998–99	Detroit	81	14	43	57	14	14
1999–2000	Detroit	81	20	53	73	19	18
2000–01	Detroit	82	15	56	71	9	18
2001–02	Detroit	78	9	50	59	13	20
2002–03	Detroit	82	18	44	62	40	38
2003–04	Detroit	81	10	28	38	19	18
2005–06	Detroit	80	16	64	80	21	50
2006–07	Detroit	80	13	49	62	40	46

Chapter Eleven

Sergei Gonchar

The Offensive Defenseman

Not viewed as one of the best defensive defensemen, Sergei Gonchar certainly makes up for his defensive deficiencies as one of the most offensive threats on any blue line in the National Hockey League. It's strange to think that he might have became a soccer player. When he was seven years old, Gonchar's favorite sport was soccer, and he loved playing down at the local field with his friends, but his father knew that he wouldn't make a good player because he ran too slowly. To replace soccer, his father introduced him to hockey, and the rest, as they say, is history.

Gonchar matured at an early age and was as much an avid reader as he was an avid hockey player. At the age of 16, while other boys were out chasing girls and watching movies, Gonchar was reading about history and philosophy, and it greatly affected his outlook on life and what he felt was important to him. "At 16, I began playing for junior teams," recalled Gonchar years later. "I traveled abroad and came to believe that if you have an opportunity to see and get to know the world, it's stupid to waste your time doing nothing."

With a strong work ethic and the drive to succeed, Gonchar found himself playing with the great Dynamo of Moscow starting in the 1992–93 season. But the Gonchar that started out with Dynamo is far different from the player we see today. The player now known for his offensive talents was then known more for his predisposition to fighting. In only 31 games in his first season with Dynamo, the defenseman earned himself 70 minutes in penalties and scored only 1 goal and 3 assists. Gonchar stayed back on the blue line and made the spot in front of the net his home, never jumping in on offensive rushes like he does today. "Now I see what I was doing wrong," said Gonchar, looking back on his mistakes. "I had learned only defensive skills, and what was most natural for me wasn't being developed."

Despite his failings, one team recognized the young Russian defenseman's natural talents. Not expecting to get drafted very high in the selection process, Gonchar was surprised when the

Washington Capitals selected him 14th overall in the 1992 NHL entry draft. The Capitals could see his potential in spite of his habit of fighting and not jumping in on the attack, and, after another year with Dynamo Moscow, he was sent to the Portland Pirates of the American Hockey League to become accustomed to the North American game.

Playing the North American style of hockey, Gonchar quickly realized he would be of better use to his team if he stopped fighting. "In America I stopped fighting for good, especially after I watched Washington tough guy Craig Berube using his fists. Then I knew I could quietly stay back."

Gonchar spent 61 games in the AHL getting used to the different style of hockey before he was called up to the Capitals during the lockout-shortened 1994–95 season. In the 31 games he played for the Capitals, Gonchar scored only 2 goals and 5 assists. He still wasn't used to the new style of play, but he was starting to fit in with his teammates, especially the ones who spoke Russian. As he got used to his surroundings off the ice, he still felt he wasn't performing up to his expectations, but all that changed when Capitals head coach Ron Wilson altered the course of the young defenseman's career.

Wilson knew that sitting back on defense was wasting Gonchar's talents. In the time leading up to the 1995–96 season, Gonchar worked hard on his offensive talents and found that he could contribute more than just a few goals to the team. When the season began, he stepped on the ice with confidence, knowing what the coach wanted him to do. Gonchar broke out of his shell that year, scoring 15 goals and 26 assists while still not neglecting his defensive duties, earning a plus/minus rating of +25. He went on to play with the Russian team in the World Cup in 1996, and the international competition helped him gain more confidence in his offensive game.

Gonchar had another good season in 1996–97, scoring 13 goals and 17 assists, but the Capitals were not at their best that year and missed out on the playoffs. Wilson knew now that he could trust Gonchar on defense and rely on his offensive talents for the Capitals' power play. Although the Capitals were a good team during the next season, no one considered them a contender in the 1998 playoffs, but with each passing round, Washington surprised Boston, Ottawa and Buffalo and made it into the finals against the Red Wings. The Red Wings were the far-better team, however, and beat the Capitals in four straight games. Gonchar was the standout player in the playoffs for the Capitals, scoring 7 goals (tied with teammates Bondra, Zednik and Juneau) and 4 assists.

In the 1998–99 season, as goal production dropped across the NHL because of an increase in defensive systems, Gonchar's goal scoring skyrocketed to record-breaking heights. At the end of the season, he had collected 21 goals, becoming the first Russian defenseman to score over 20 goals during the regular season—and he did it in only 53 games, forced to sit out a large part of the season because of injury. His amazing offensive feats continued through the next few seasons, racking up a career high in 2001–02 with 26 goals and 33 assists. They were the kind of stats that could get a defenseman a nomination for the Norris Trophy, but he was continually overlooked because of his perceived weakness on the defensive end of his game.

While Gonchar's stats soared, the Capitals' fortunes fluctuated with each season, from 102 points at the end of the 1999–2000 season to missing the playoffs just two years later. After 10 seasons with the Capitals and still no Stanley Cup, Gonchar knew it was time to pick up, move cities and hope for a fresh start with a new team. Halfway through the 2003–04 season, he was traded to the Boston Bruins, a young team with high hopes. But an early exit in the playoffs disappointed him. The Bruins management was looking for a defenseman who could lead the team. They wanted the reincarnation of Bobby Orr, and Gonchar, although talented, did not fit in their future plans. During the lockout season of 2004–05, Gonchar spent his time with the Russian team Metallurg Magnitogorsk, keeping fit for the eventual return of the game. It was during this time off that Gonchar found himself on the move again, this time joining another young, hopeful team, the Pittsburgh Penguins.

The Penguins hoped that Gonchar's experience on defense could help lead young guys like Sidney Crosby, Jordan Staal and Evgeni Malkin. Mario Lemieux was no longer part of the team, and the Penguins needed a calm mind to take hold in the dressing room. Although no one on the Penguins team wore the captain's C after Mario Lemieux retired, Gonchar became one of the defacto leaders of the team. In his two seasons with the Penguins, he had to sit out a few games because of injury, but when he was on the ice, he remained a scoring threat and could always be found on the point during power plays. But don't count out this veteran defenseman just yet, for he has a few good years of hockey left in his skates.

Season	Team	GP	Goals	Assists	Points	+/-	Penalties
1994–95	Washington	31	2	5	7	4	22
1995–96	Washington	78	15	26	41	25	60
1996–97	Washington	57	13	17	30	–11	36
1997–98	Washington	72	5	16	21	2	66
1998–99	Washington	53	21	10	31	1	57
1999–2000	Washington	73	18	36	54	26	52
2000–01	Washington	76	19	38	57	12	70
2001–02	Washington	76	26	33	59	–1	58
2002–03	Washington	82	18	49	67	13	52
2003–04	Washington	56	7	42	49	–20	44
2003–04	Boston	15	4	5	9	6	12
2005–06	Pittsburgh	75	12	46	58	–13	100
2006–07	Pittsburgh	82	13	54	67	–5	72

Chapter Twelve

Sergei Zubov

The Secret Weapon

The modern National Hockey League player is the pinnacle of athleticism after a lifetime of training the mind and body to perform at its highest level. How then, does the best defenseman on the Dallas Stars smoke a pack of cigarettes a day? It seems counterintuitive for a professional athlete to smoke a cigarette before a game, and even between periods, but Sergei Zubov's habit hasn't yet interfered with his play, and he consistently logs the most ice time among defensemen on his team.

Hailing from Moscow, Russia, Zubov first burst onto the scene playing for the old Soviet Union super team, the Central Red Army, between 1988 and 1992. Although he racked up only 17 goals in his four years with the Red Army, Zubov was a solid defenseman who could always be relied on for his vision of the ice and puck-handling abilities. He knew that he could contribute much more in terms of offense, but with a team rife with scoring talent such as Pavel Bure and Sergei Fedorov, Zubov's offensive talents were not really needed. As the Red Army's top young defenseman, Zubov represented his country in the 1989 and 1990 World Junior Championship, winning the gold and silver medals, respectively. After the fall of the Soviet Union, the hockey team remained partially intact, and Zubov quarterbacked the defense of the Russian team to a silver medal in the 1992 Winter Olympics in Albertville, France.

The New York Rangers were the first NHL team to take interest in the young Russian defenseman, scouting him prior to the 1990 NHL entry draft. They admired his ability to play solid defense at such a young age and to read the way a play would develop on the ice, knowing when to jump in on the offense and when to hang back. After several rounds in the draft, the New York Rangers were surprised that Zubov was still available, and they were able to select him 85th overall. After two more years in the Russian hockey system, Zubov was assigned to the Ranger's farm team in Binghamton for the start of the 1992–93 American Hockey League season. Zubov immediately made an impact, scoring 7 goals and 29 assists in 30 games. After making his mark in the minors, the New York Rangers knew that Zubov was ready to make the jump to the professional ranks. He joined the Rangers halfway through the season and fit in immediately on the team, scoring 8 goals and 23 assists in his NHL debut season. But as good as Zubov was, it wasn't enough to propel the Rangers into the playoffs, and they finished the 1992–93 season with only 79 points overall. The rookie was a little disappointed that he didn't get into the post-season, but he wouldn't have to wait long before he got the chance of his career just one season later.

In 1993–94, his second season with the Rangers, Zubov was already one of the better offensive defensemen in the league, racking up a career high of 12 goals and 77 assists, for 89 points. The Rangers went into the playoffs as one of the best teams, wanting to prove themselves after missing the 1993 playoffs. They easily handled the New York Islanders in the first round of the playoff run, sweeping them in four straight games before another easy series against the Washington Capitals. Things got interesting in the conference finals when Zubov and the Rangers came head to head with the New Jersey Devils. The Devils had a good team, but more importantly, they had the young goaltending phenomenon Martin Brodeur, who was surpassing all expectations in the playoffs. It was to no one's surprise that after five games, the Devils found themselves in an enviable position with a 3–2 series lead over a stifled Rangers squad, whose scoring lines had been shut down by the stand-on-your-head acrobatics of Brodeur. But captain Mark Messier would not let his team get down. He rallied his teammates and led the charge as the Rangers came back and won the series. In the finals, the team was in tough against the Canucks' high-powered offense, but Zubov and his defensive partners managed to keep the series very close. The Rangers were able to hold it together to win a nail-biter of a game seven with a final score of 3–2 for the team's first Stanley Cup victory in 54 years. Zubov contributed 5 goals and 14 assists. It was the young Russian defenseman's first taste of NHL glory, and he was only in his sophomore season.

Zubov returned to the Rangers' lineup for the 1994–95 regular-season campaign and was having a great year with, 10 goals and 26 assists in only 38 games, but there were rumors of discontent in the Rangers' dressing room. Only those involved know for sure what happened, but so the rumors go: Messier and Zubov did not agree on a long list of things and were disrupting the harmony of the dressing room. So the young defenseman was sent packing to the Pittsburgh

Penguins, along with Petr Nedved, for Luc Robitaille and Ulf Samuelsson.

Zubov was a good fit with the high-powered offense of the Pittsburgh Penguins, scoring 11 goals and 55 assists in 1995–96. Because of his strong skating and superb stick-handling skills, the Penguins used Zubov often on the power play, and he was an asset to the team defensively as they moved through the 1996 playoffs. But the honeymoon between Zubov and the Penguins did not last very long after they were eliminated in the conference finals by the Florida Panthers in the seventh game. The Penguins spent the off-season trying to figure out what they needed to do to prevent another early exit from the playoffs when they were one of the teams expected to go all the way to the finals. Penguins management came up with the notion that they needed size on defense, and although Zubov had 14 assists in the playoffs, he was deemed expendable and traded to the Dallas Stars for the towering defenseman Kevin Hatcher.

After four years in the National Hockey League, Zubov was already on his third team, but with the Dallas Stars, he finally found a home for his talents. Under the system of Dallas head coach Ken Hitchcock, Zubov's artistry with the puck, both on offense and defense, was well used and exploited. In the more offensive-minded Western Conference, Zubov had more room on the ice to start his rushes and make his crisp outlet passes to the advancing forwards. The Stars, however, were one of the more defense-oriented teams in the West, and Zubov was expected to be solid on the blue line as well. This double duty never bothered the wily Russian; he actually flourished in it, knowing for the first time in his career what his role was on his team. In his first season with the Stars, he scored 13 goals, and his 30 assists led all defensemen across the NHL.

Whether the arrival of Zubov was responsible for the Stars' turnaround or not can't be known for certain, but the season before his arrival, the Stars were at the bottom of the Central Division, finishing the season with only 66 points. Just one season later, after Zubov's arrival, the Stars jumped straight to first place in their division with 104 points and earned a spot in the playoffs. The Stars were eliminated in the first round of the playoffs in a thrilling game-seven overtime loss to the Edmonton Oilers; however, they had started to build a solid team around a core defensive group led by the talents of Sergei Zubov.

After another good season in 1997–98 with 57 points in the regular season and a playoff run that ended just two wins short of a spot in the finals, things took a turn for the worse off the ice for Zubov in June 1998. The normally quiet, unassuming Russian defenseman was arrested for allegedly assaulting his wife, Irina, and threatening her with a knife shortly after the Stars' elimination from the playoffs. Zubov avoided any further public embarrassment when a Dallas grand jury declined to indict him after his wife refused to go through with the charges. After a horrible summer, Zubov returned to the Stars' training camp for the 1998–99 season, more determined than ever to prove his commitment to the team.

While Zubov's talents could not be denied, critics of the game always pointed to one aspect of his style that kept him from being considered one of the best defensemen in the game. At six feet, one inch tall and 210 pounds, Zubov is an average size for an NHL player, but it was how he used his size that bothered critics so much. Although he didn't take many penalties (only a career high of 46 minutes in the 2005–06 season), Zubov was often physically dominated by bigger players in corners and would turn over the puck in his own zone. It was an aspect of his game that he was always trying to improve, but when weighed against his litany of other skills, it was a minor flaw. Dallas head coach Ken Hitchcock singled Zubov out for that exact flaw in the final games of the 1998–99 regular season, saying, "No. He has to be a better player for us. He hasn't been effective on the power play. He's just been okay."

Zubov got the hint and turned on the afterburners for the remaining games and the start of the playoffs. When the playoffs got underway, the Dallas Stars were well prepared to face any challenge thrown at them and got their first test against the team that had eliminated them in the first round just two seasons ago. The Oilers were no challenge this time for Dallas and were taken out easily in four straight games. The series against the St. Louis Blues was a little tighter, with four games going into overtime, but the Dallas defense was just too strong, and the Blues fell in six games. The Stars could feel that their focus on defense was working and frustrating their opponents at every turn.

Things were more difficult against the Colorado Avalanche in the conference finals. The Avalanche had powerful offensive weapons in players such as Joe Sakic and Peter Forsberg and arguably the best-ever goaltender in Patrick Roy. With each game, it became apparent that the teams were evenly matched and the series could go to either team, but the Stars' defense made the difference in the seventh game, keeping the Avalanche down to only 1 goal.

The Stars were in for a challenge in the final series against the equally defensive Buffalo Sabres and the goaltending of Dominik Hasek, but the Stars felt that the Sabres could be matched and defeated if the Stars stuck to their system. Although it wasn't the most exciting series, the Stars' defense was able to stifle the Buffalo forwards to win the Stanley Cup in six games. Zubov contributed with 1 goal and 12 assists and collected the second Stanley Cup of his NHL career.

After performing beyond expectations, Zubov was offered a contract extension into the 2004–05 season by Dallas Stars general manager Bob Gainey, securing one of the most underrated defensemen in the league. "His performance for our hockey club over the past four years has been exemplary," said Gainey.

Zubov had a home in the NHL and was not about to give up on one of the more successful clubs in the league. "It's really exciting for myself and my family," Zubov told the media after signing the contract. "We've spent four years over here; so far it's just a great time with the team. I've been concentrating more on just playing hockey, but it's great to get back with one of the best teams again."

For much of his career, Zubov was the silent star on the blue line, making little plays and quick decisions that sometimes make the difference between a win or a loss. His talent was always overlooked, and he constantly missed out during the NHL awards. Zubov finally received some recognition when he was nominated for the Norris Trophy after a stellar 2005–06 season, in which he scored 71 points and had a plus/minus rating of +20, but he was passed over for perennial favorite Nicklas Lidstrom. Still, there is no longer any doubt in hockey circles that Zubov has earned the distinction as one of the best defensemen in the league. He is currently the only active defenseman to have scored over 40 points in 10 consecutive seasons, and his plus/minus rating rarely drops into the negatives. And he still smokes! But someday it will catch up to him.

Season	Team	GP	Goals	Assists	Points	+/-	Penalties
1992–93	NY Rangers	49	8	23	31	–1	4
1993–94	NY Rangers	78	12	77	89	20	39
1994–95	NY Rangers	38	10	26	36	–2	18
1995–96	Pittsburgh	64	11	55	66	28	22
1996–97	Dallas	78	13	30	43	19	24
1997–98	Dallas	73	10	47	57	16	16
1998–99	Dallas	81	10	41	51	9	20
1999–2000	Dallas	77	9	33	42	–2	18
2000–01	Dallas	79	10	41	51	22	24
2001–02	Dallas	80	12	32	44	–4	22
2002–03	Dallas	82	11	44	55	21	26
2003–04	Dallas	77	7	35	42	0	20
2005–06	Dallas	78	13	58	71	20	46
2006–07	Dallas	78	12	42	54	0	26

Chapter Thirteen

Andrei Markov

The Quiet One

When he joined the Montréal Canadiens for the 2000–01 season, few people knew who he was, and his teammates had trouble getting to know him, given that he did not speak a word of either English or French. A man of very few words, Andrei Markov let his game do the talking in his first season in the National Hockey League, and in the following five seasons, he made a place for himself as one of the best defensemen in the league.

The steep climb to the professional ranks began in a world far different from the streets of Montréal and the lights of the Bell Centre. Born on December 20, 1979, in Voskresensk, Russia—a city of about 95,000 people located 50 miles from Moscow—Markov began his hockey life at the age of eight, when his parents took him to a hockey school whose most famous graduate was Igor Larionov. Most people would never know that the city of Voskresensk existed if it weren't one of the best producers of Russian hockey talent, including such players as Sergei Berezin, Valerie Zelepukin, Igor Larionov, Vyacheslav Kozlov and Valeri Kamensky. Markov took to hockey immediately, but it wasn't the only sport he loved to play. It might surprise Markov fans today because he is so quiet and unassuming on the ice, but as a young man, he enjoyed boxing down at the local gym. Markov even dropped out of hockey school to pursue his other interests in sports, but he quickly found that hockey was his one true passion. Since then, he has never looked back.

As a teenager, Markov, like most his age, wanted to play forward and score the goals that could get the crowd into the games, and though he did not have the goal-scoring touch he would need to make him a feared sniper, his skills as a forward were good enough for the young Russian to break into the local elite professional squad with Khimik Voskresensk. The Khimik coach recognized in Markov's first season with the team that at the higher level, the player's offensive skills were not good enough to merit enough ice time. During the off-season, the coach worked with Markov at switching his playing attitude from a center to a blue liner. This simple switch to defense changed the future professional path for the young Russian. Markov proved adept at his defensive duties. He was good at reading how a play would develop and knowing when to pinch in to stop a rush and when to back off and retreat to protect the net. But with years of training as a forward, Markov could also be relied on to support his teammates on the attack.

As a result of his newfound success on the point, Markov caught the attention of the national junior hockey organizers, who quickly found him a spot on the team for the 1997 tournament. Markov's aspirations of international gold in his first year were dashed when the Russian squad ended the tournament in third place, good enough for bronze. After another year of gaining experience, Markov was invited back to the World Juniors in 1998 and was named a tournament all-star for his efforts. Despite the personal glory given to Markov, he had to settle for the silver medal this time after a heartbreaking loss to the Finnish team.

Markov, however, would not hang his head for long. The international tournament was the perfect showcase for the Russian defenseman's talents, and it wasn't long before the National Hockey League scouts came knocking at his door. One team in particular was so impressed with Markov's talents that they set their sights on him during the 1998 NHL entry draft. The Montréal Canadiens had long had a revolving door on the blue line, and to make any inroads in the playoffs, they would need a reliable man on the point who would add some much-needed offense on power plays and five-on-five situations. Markov was still around by the time the Canadiens used their sixth pick, and they chose him 162nd overall.

The Montréal Canadiens were eager to get Markov in their organization and begin the process of adapting him to the North American game, but Markov, not wanting to jump directly into the league, thought he still needed some work before making the big move to the NHL. The same summer he was drafted by the Montréal Canadiens, he signed with the equally historic Russian superclub, Dynamo Moscow of the Russian Superligue, under a two-year contract. The Canadiens organization was not pleased by the delay, but Markov felt that it would be a better fit in his life and career to stay in Russia and develop further.

With Dynamo Moscow, Markov developed under the tutelage of head coach Zinetula Bilyaletdinov and became one of the best defensive players in the league. In his first season with the club, Markov tallied 10 goals and 11 assists in 38 games, finishing as one of the top-scoring defensemen in the league. For his efforts on the blue line, the Superligue awarded Markov the Golden Helmet Award as the Most Valuable Player. The Montréal Canadiens did not give up in their pursuit of the young Russian and tried once again to lure him to the National Hockey League after his impressive first season in the Superligue, but Markov still felt he wasn't yet ready to make the big move, and he still had a year left on his contract with Dynamo to fulfill. So the Canadiens patiently folded their arms and waited for Markov to come to them.

Markov's second and final year under contract with Dynamo was by far the most successful season in his career. He scored 11 goals and 12 assists, for 23 points in 29 games, leading all defensemen in scoring. His accomplishments earned him the title of best defenseman in the league and another Golden Helmet Award. With the best defenseman in the Russian Superligue, Dynamo finished as regular season champions; the playoffs, however, were not as kind to Markov's team. Everything was rolling along fine until the finals, when Dynamo Moscow met rival Metallurg Magnitogorsk.

Markov's team found themselves down by one goal with a few seconds remaining in the game. On the bench, the Dynamo players hung their heads at having come so close to winning the Superligue title. Markov was on the ice in the final moments of the game and had the puck behind his own net with just seconds on the clock, when he decided to shoot the puck down the ice as a last act of desperation. He let go an innocent-looking high slap shot that traveled the length of the ice and beat a very surprised and embarrassed Metallurg goaltender on the glove side. The goal tied the game at 1–1 and sent a wave of life through the Dynamo players. Unfortunately, their good luck ran out in the overtime period, and they had to return to their dressing rooms while the Metallurg players celebrated their championship win.

The summer of 2000 was a difficult one for Markov. He left behind his beloved Russia and his parents and sister in his hometown, but there was also the added isolation of being in a new country, not knowing the language (or, in the case of Montréal, languages) and not knowing the culture. The move to Montréal was like starting over again for the young Russian, but it had always been his dream to play in the National Hockey League against the best players in the world. He knew that if he could prove himself in the NHL, then he would have truly made it as a professional hockey player.

The Canadiens realized that the transition would be difficult for Markov, so he was roomed with Gino Odjick, who had learned a bit of Russian when he played for the Vancouver Canucks and was good friends with Pavel Bure. But things were still not all that easy. The rookie had difficulty adjusting to the North American game, with a smaller ice surface and a lot more contact. Although Markov had his girlfriend with him in Montréal, he really missed his family and friends.

To get his mind off the huge cultural change, he focused solely on hockey. But as a rookie, his ice time was limited to around 10 to 15 minutes per game, and sometimes he was not even dressed for several games. Frustrated at not receiving the ice time and respect for his skills that he thought he deserved, Markov seriously contemplated returning to Russia. He could not speak the language, he wasn't getting the ice time, and the Canadiens finished at the bottom of their division, failing to make the playoffs. But the call of the National Hockey League was too strong for Markov to resist. The thrill of playing in the best league in the world against players like Mario Lemieux, Jaromir Jagr and Joe Sakic kept him from returning home. He had finally made it to the NHL, and he wasn't about to give up on his dream because he was a little homesick.

This is the kind of passion and drive that the Canadiens scouts recognized in Markov when they first signed him and that they continued to count on as he became the best defenseman on the team. "He plays with a lot of drive. He sees the ice very well," said Canadiens scout Trevor Timmins. "He moves the puck very effectively and he's got a great shot."

In his first season, Markov impressed the Canadiens with 6 goals and 17 assists in 63 games, then improved on his point totals in his sophomore season with 5 goals and 19 assists in just 56 games. But it was in the 2002 playoffs that Markov truly dazzled Canadiens management and earned himself a permanent spot with the team.

Barely squeaking into the playoffs, the Canadiens were not expected to make it past their first-round opponents, the Boston Bruins. The Bruins had finished the season second overall in the league and were riding high on the back of goaltender Byron Defoe. The Canadiens were expected to go down rather quickly, but the long history of animosity between the two teams ensured an entertaining series for fans. Montréal traded wins with the Bruins, and after four games, the series was tied with two wins apiece. The last two games of the series were tight defensive affairs, with Markov stepping up to his potential and frustrating the Bruins offense at every turn. His success in the series came from his vision of the ice and his ability to see how the opponent's play would develop. Time and time again, Markov would anticipate a pass or a rush, intercept the puck and send his teammates in on the rush. With Markov on the blue line, the Canadiens won the next two games and advanced to the conference semi-finals against the Carolina Hurricanes.

The Canadiens were in tough against the Hurricanes, with many players nursing injuries from the end of the regular season and the first series against the Bruins, but Montréal held on and split the first four games against Carolina. By game five, however, the Canadiens had run out of steam, and no matter what Markov could contribute, he could not stop the Hurricanes from running them over in the final two games.

Despite the early exit, the Canadiens management was impressed enough with Markov's play to give him a full-time position on the Canadiens blue line. The trust the team put in Markov paid off, with the 2002–03 season turning out to be his best to date. Markov played in 79 full games, recording a career high of 13 goals and 24 assists, for 37 points, and, most importantly, his plus/minus rating was +13. The plus/minus rating was all the more impressive given that the Canadiens finished the season with a losing record and once again missed the playoffs.

Markov's stock continued to rise as the next season got underway. The Canadiens finished the year with a respectable 93 points and a place in the playoffs. Markov had another good season, with 6 goals and 22 assists, but the Russian defenseman played in only 69 games because of injuries throughout the season. His importance to the team was clearly illustrated when he was not playing, as the team's winning percentage dropped. It's difficult to say for certain whether Markov's absence was a major factor in the Canadiens' losing games while he was injured, but there is no doubt that he was a major contributor to the team's overall confidence and success.

With Markov back in the lineup for the playoffs, the Canadiens made another push for the Cup, beating back the Boston Bruins in an exciting seven-game series. But once again, Markov's hopes of winning the Stanley Cup were dashed when the Canadiens were eliminated in the second round by the eventual champions, the Tampa Bay Lightning.

When the NHL lockout occurred in what was to be the 2004–05 season, Markov returned without hesitation to his old Russian Superligue team,

Dynamo Moscow. Playing in 42 of 60 games, Markov was back in his comfort zone and had a great season with his old club. In his 42 games, he finished as the top defenseman on the team, with 23 points, and quarterbacked the team to the top spot in the league. When the National Hockey League and the Players' Association finally settled their differences, Markov returned to the Canadiens lineup better than ever. It seemed that returning to Russian soil for a full year did him some good and focused his defensive skills as one of the veteran defensemen on the team.

Markov achieved a career high of 46 points for the 2005–06 season, playing in only 67 regular season games. His skills on the blue line helped the Canadiens squeak into the playoffs with 93 points, good enough for seventh place overall. But the eventual champions, the Carolina Hurricanes, spoiled Markov's banner year, eliminating the Canadiens in the first round in six games.

In 2006–07, Markov had a career year as the top defensive defenseman on the team. He ended the season with a respectable 6 goals and 43 assists, but it was his solid defensive contribution to the team that made him such a valuable asset. His teammate Sheldon Souray may get all the attention as the Canadiens' top defenseman because of his offensive talents (26 goals and

38 assists), but Souray had one of the worst plus/minus ratings on the team, with –28, while Markov finished with a +2 rating.

The Montréal Canadiens management had some serious questions to ask themselves during the off-season in regard to their defensive core. Markov became an unrestricted free agent at the end of the season and was going to command a hefty salary when it came to re-signing his contract. The Canadiens wanted him enough to put their faith in the Russian defenseman down on paper, and they re-signed Markov to a multi-year, multimillion-dollar contract, ensuring that the young defenseman will be a large part of the Canadiens' future successes.

Season	Team	GP	Goals	Assists	Points	+/-	Penalties
2000–01	Montréal	63	6	17	23	–6	18
2001–02	Montréal	56	5	19	24	–1	24
2002–03	Montréal	79	13	24	37	13	34
2003–04	Montréal	69	6	22	28	–2	20
2005–06	Montréal	67	10	36	46	13	74
2006–07	Montréal	77	6	43	49	2	56

Chapter Fourteen

Jay Bouwmeester

The Veteran Youngster

It is rare to make a first appearance in the National Hockey League at the age of 18, but Jay Bouwmeester, born on September 27, 1983, is not ordinary. Hockey players always have a story about when they first put on a pair of skates, and most say they were around the age of five or six. The term "natural" is not applied to many players, but because Bouwmeester first took to skating at the tender age of two years, it is hard to find another word to describe this six-foot-four-inch, 210-pound tour de force.

Throughout his development into an NHL player, Bouwmeester's loyal parents were by his side, helping him to become one of the best young defensemen in the game. His father, Dan, did not enroll the young prodigy in organized hockey until Jay was six, preferring instead to work with his young son on the fundamentals of the game so when his son did join a team, he would be able to skate circles around kids his age. Jay's father was by his son's side through most of his youth hockey career, and it helped keep the young star grounded. "Both my parents were very supportive growing up, and that's something I'm really thankful for," said Bouwmeester in an interview with writer Jeff Rudd.

The investments made by his parents began to pay off as young Bouwmeester started to get noticed by leagues and teams across North America, which all needed to add a player of his size and caliber. Barely had he reached the age of 14 when player agents began calling the Bouwmeester home in Edmonton, Alberta, to express interest in representing the talented defenseman. He moved up to the Western Hockey League after being drafted in 1998 by the Medicine Hat Tigers. Bouwmeester had many options before him, including going into the U.S. college market, but at 15 years old, he wanted to stay as close to home as possible.

In his first year with the Medicine Hat Tigers, he played just eight games, but after settling into his new life, Bouwmeester adapted to the new level of play and was soon one of the dominant defensemen in the WHL. The Tigers were the perfect team for Bouwmeester to cut his proverbial teeth with, having a history of producing talented players such as Trevor Linden and Lanny McDonald. Unfortunately, Linden and McDonald were no longer on Bouwmeester's team, and the Tigers went through three consecutive losing seasons, missing the playoffs each of the four years he was on the team.

His stats during his three years with the Tigers show marked improvement. Playing eight games in 1998–1999, he scored only 2 goals and 1 assist, but in 1999–2000, playing in all 64 league games, he improved to 13 goals and 21 assists, for 34 points. Not content with resting on his laurels, Bouwmeester improved once again in 2000–2001, with 14 goals and 39 assists, for 53 points, and had his best season in 2001–2002, with 11 goals and 50 assists.

Despite his team's disappointing performances, Bouwmeester was one of the lone standouts on the Tigers. He worked hard on the fundamentals of the game and on building his strength, and it paid off with each successive season. His skating ability was his prime weapon. For a player towering on the ice at six feet, four inches, he had a natural flow, something many players of his size just didn't, and he combined his skating abilities with the puck movement skills of a forward. Bouwmeester's stats may have been much better had his team not needed him so much on the blue line. But that is what made the statistics he did earn all the more impressive. His abilities earned him a spot on the Canadian team for the 2000 World Junior Championship. At only 16 years old, he was the youngest player ever selected to the team. Unfortunately, he did not come home with the gold medal, settling instead for the bronze.

With three successful seasons and international experience under his belt, Bouwmeester was one of the players expected to go in the top three at the 2002 NHL entry draft held at Toronto's Air Canada Centre. The Florida Panthers held the first pick in the draft and were looking to shore up their defense with a big, skilled defenseman. The Columbus Blue Jackets held the third pick and wanted to ensure they would get the top-scoring prospect of the London Knights, left-winger Rick Nash, so they made a deal with the Panthers: Florida agreed to switch positions in the draft in return for a promise that Columbus would not select Bouwmeester. In making the deal, the Blue Jackets jumped ahead of the Atlanta Thrashers, who had the second pick, and were able to select Nash, while Florida happily selected Bouwmeester third overall.

While some players commit most of their years to hockey and never make it to the bright lights of the National Hockey League, Bouwmeester seemed predestined to play for an NHL team since the first day he laced up a pair of skates. He wasn't chosen number one, but it was only the deal struck with Columbus that kept him from this bonus distinction. Either way, it didn't matter to Bouwmeester because he now had his chance. In just a few months, Bouwmeester's life changed considerably, from a life living with his parents and taking buses to a life in sunny Florida in his own condominium and taking chartered jets all across North America.

At training camp, Florida management and coaches began to realize what level of player they had signed to the team. "Bouwmeester has a unique combination of hockey sense, skating ability and stick skills," said assistant coach Paul Baxter in Jeff Rudd's book *Hockey's Young Superstars*. "You know, this is my 29th year in professional hockey, and I've never seen an 18-year-old who's got the complete package like him. He seems to be at the 26- or 27-year-old level, and I'm not talking about average players, I'm talking top players. He's been like that since training camp."

Normally, teams would not take a chance on unproven 18-year-old players, preferring to keep them in the minors to work on their game rather than ruin their confidence at the pro level. But

Bouwmeester was performing above and beyond the expectations of the Florida coaches, especially for a defenseman. Most hockey professionals agree that the job of a defenseman at the pro level usually takes several years to master and feel comfortable with, but Bouwmeester was so relaxed in his attitude and confident in his abilities that it didn't matter whether he was playing against other 18-year-olds or 35-year-old seasoned NHL veterans.

Without the fanfare that would have welcomed him in any Canadian city, Bouwmeester began his NHL career with the Florida Panthers at the start of the 2002–03 NHL season. However, as a top draft pick, Bouwmeester had joined a team that had been struggling throughout much of its brief history and did not have a veteran defenseman to help guide the young rookie through his first season. The team suffered through a disappointing season, with 24 wins, 36 losses and 13 ties, and Bouwmeester's numbers reflected the state of the team around him, with a plus/minus rating of –29 by season's end. Few could blame the young rookie for the disappointing season, but Bouwmeester was not happy with his performance and worked even harder during the off-season to improve his game.

He impressed enough people during his first season to be invited to play on the Canadian men's national hockey team for the 2003 World Championship, held in Helsinki, Finland. The international game suited Bouwmeester perfectly: the extra room on the ice allowed him to employ his excellent skating abilities to move the puck up the ice to start forward rushes and then get back on defense, matching skating with the speedy European players. He put 7 points up on the score board during the tournament and was a major contributor to the team's defensive success. He was important enough to be named the tournament's top defenseman while helping his teammates to the gold medal.

Despite another bad season for the Panthers in 2003–04, Bouwmeester improved on the ice with 20 points and a plus/minus rating of –15 in 61 games. Despite the rating, he was still one of the top defensemen on the team and regularly logged over 20 minutes of ice time per game. During the lockout of 2004–05, he spent time in the American Hockey League keeping fit to be ready for the return of the NHL regular schedule. When hockey finally returned, Bouwmeester was ready to prove he could be a leader on the team and one of the best defensemen in the league. On the international scene, he again helped the national hockey team win gold at the World Championship with another solid performance, but no top defenseman award this time.

Although the Florida Panthers continued to struggle to put numbers up in the win column, Bouwmeester managed to more than double his points from 20 to 46 and went from a plus/minus rating of –15 to +1. They aren't the stats of the best defenseman in the league, but when his team is considered, his stats start to look a little different. The few detractors who criticized Bouwmeester obviously failed to see the innate skill in him.

When historians write of Jay Bouwmeester's days in the National Hockey League, they will most likely pinpoint the 2006–07 season as the year he came into his own and became one of the top defensemen in the league, with 12 goals, 30 assists and a plus/minus rating of +23. He received the honor of participating in the All-Star game that year as well, and if things keep going in the upward direction for Bouwmeester, he will surely one day be holding the Stanley Cup high above his head.

Season	Team	GP	Goals	Assists	Points	+/-	Penalties
2002–03	Florida	82	4	12	16	-29	14
2003–04	Florida	61	2	18	20	-15	30
2005–06	Florida	82	5	41	46	1	79
2006–07	Florida	82	12	30	42	23	66

Chapter Fifteen

Future Stars

Marc-André Bergeron

Marc-André Bergeron had many people talking during his days in the Québec Major Junior Hockey League as one of the new breed of defensemen that the league was looking for as changes to the rules were being discussed to open up the scoring in the game. At just five feet, 10 inches tall, Bergeron was not looked on as a defenseman that could make it under the old system in the NHL, but when the rule changes were established after the NHL returned from the lockout season, a player of his size and offensive-minded play was highly sought after.

Despite scoring 24 goals and 50 assists in the 1999–2000 season, during his third year in the QMJHL with the Shawinigan Cataractes, followed by an incredible fourth year, in which he scored 42 goals and 59 assists, Bergeron was passed over in the 1999 NHL entry draft. There were a few interested teams, but as sometimes happens in the National Hockey League, talented players can be overlooked. But in 2001, the Edmonton Oilers took a second look at the young defenseman and signed him as a free agent. It was his chance to make it into the big league, and he knew he had to make an immediate impression on the Oilers management; after all, general manager Kevin Lowe had been a defenseman and had played with other greats such as Paul Coffey.

Bergeron joined the Hamilton Bulldogs in the AHL for further conditioning and worked heavily on his defensive skills. He got his first chance in the NHL during the 2002–03 season, playing in five games and scoring 1 goal and 1 assist. The Oilers were impressed enough to have him return for the 2003–04 season, and in 54 games, he scored a respectable 9 goals and 17 assists. He quickly endeared himself to the Oilers' faithful fans, who were always looking to relive the glory of the 1980s, with his exciting end-to-end rushes, which reminded them of the legendary moves of former Oiler Paul Coffey. Bergeron, not exactly the biggest player on the ice, wasn't expected to play a very physical game, but when he delivered an open-ice hip check to Dallas Stars forward

Brendan Morrow during the 2003 playoffs, the Oilers knew they had a special player.

When the league tightened its control on hooking and opened up the game to the faster skaters, Bergeron showed the skills that made him one of the highest-scoring defensemen in the QMJHL. In the 2005–06 season, Bergeron scored 15 goals and 20 assists and was instrumental in the team's success in getting into the playoffs and making it all the way to the finals against the Carolina Hurricanes. But one small error in the first game of the series wiped away the progress made during the regular and post-season.

During the Oilers' 2006 run to the finals, much of the credit for keeping the team in the running went to their goaltender, Dwayne Roloson. He on more than one occasion made more than 40 saves per game to keep his team alive in the face of more powerful teams such as the Detroit Red Wings in round one, and it was Roloson whom the Oilers were counting on to take them to the championship. But near the end of game one of the finals, the Oilers' high hopes suddenly came crashing down. As time wound down, Hurricanes forward Andrew Ladd tried to crash in front of the net, and Bergeron attemped to steer him clear of the goal, but the two players ended up crashing into Roloson, causing him to injure his leg and have to sit out the remainder of the series. Many fans and sportswriters blamed Bergeron for steering the Carolina player into Roloson and ruining their chances at winning the Stanley Cup. With that disastrous ending to his excellent season, Bergeron could sense his days in an Oilers uniform were numbered, and halfway through the 2006–07 season, he was traded to the New York Islanders.

The Islanders made a good deal for the young, speedy defenseman with a natural ability with the puck and a blistering slap shot that was once recorded at 102 miles per hour. If he can remain healthy and consistent in his play, he will surely be a defenseman to look out for in the future.

Season	Team	GP	Goals	Assists	Points	+/–	Penalties
2002–03	Edmonton	5	1	1	2	2	9
2003–04	Edmonton	54	9	17	26	13	26
2005–06	Edmonton	75	15	20	35	3	38
2006–07	Edmonton	55	8	17	25	–9	28
2006–07	NY Islanders	23	6	15	21	5	10

Brian Campbell

Growing up in a small Ontario town, Brian Campbell was like millions of other young Canadian boys who dreamed of making it into the National Hockey League. His skating ability and vision of the ice made him a natural for a position on defense, and ever since his bantam days, he has remained on the blue line. His strong defensive skills and ability to move the puck out of the zone got him noticed by the Ottawa 67's of the Ontario Hockey League, and he was selected in the third round of the 1995 OHL draft.

Campbell had a decent start in his rookie year with the 67's, scoring a respectable 27 points in 66 games. But after one season of getting used to the speed of play and harder physical treatment, he adjusted his game and never took a step back. With each passing season, he increased his point totals, and his defensive vision on the ice grew stronger. He also earned himself a good reputation for delivering devastating hits to unsuspecting players who crossed into his zone with their heads down or away from the play.

After a second good year with the 67's, increasing his point totals to 7 goals and 36 assists, Campbell was on many teams' lists by the time the 1997 NHL entry draft came around. The only thing against him was his small size compared to some of the big players coming out of the minors. But the Buffalo Sabres were willing to take a chance on the red-headed defenseman and selected him 156th overall. The Sabres recognized a good player when they saw one, and they knew with a little work and a few more pounds, he could be one of the best in the league. They were pleased that Campbell finished his final season with the Ottawa 67's with 12 goals and 75 assists, for 87 points, the most of any player that year on his team. For his efforts, the OHL honored him with the Red Tilson Trophy as the league's most outstanding player, the Max Kaminsky Trophy as the defenseman of the year and the William Hanley Trophy as the league's most gentlemanly player, with the icing on the cake coming from the Canadian Hockey League, which gave him the Player of the Year Award.

The Sabres were eager to get the young defensive phenomenon into the NHL, but they felt he needed one more year with the team's AHL affiliate, the Rochester Americans, to make sure he was ready for the big league. For the next two years, Campbell bounced between the AHL and the NHL, playing in only 20 games with the Sabres in that time. Not that he wasn't performing up to standard, but the Sabres were full with defensemen, and it wasn't until the 2001–02 season that he became a permanent member on the team. However, permanent did not mean regular. Buffalo head coach Lindy Ruff was still unsure of the young defenseman's abilities to perform at a consistent rate and often sat him out for games during the next few seasons.

Campbell and other smaller, mobile defensemen like him around the league broke out of their shells when the league changed its rules before the start of the 2005–06 season after the lockout. Opening up the game allowed players like Campbell to commit more openly to offensive rushes, and by the end of that season, he had showed the Sabres management the talent that got him noticed in the first place. In 79 games, the speedy defenseman scored a career of high of 12 goals and 32 assists, but with the sacrifice of his plus/minus rating, which fell to a disappointing –14. Despite his flaws, Campbell was a big part of the Sabres' push for the Cup in the 2006 playoffs. Anyone who had questioned his lack of physical play quickly took it back after the devastating hit he delivered on the Philadelphia Flyers' R.J. Umberger in the first round. It was a brutal but clean check that knocked Umberger to the ice unconscious with a concussion.

The Sabres were eventually eliminated in a thrilling seven-game series in the conference finals against the Carolina Hurricanes, so Campbell returned for the 2006–07 season with the drive to improve his defensive skills for a more well-rounded approach to his position. He knew he had established his name as one of the top defensemen in the league when he was voted first among all Eastern Conference defensemen in All-Star voting. Campbell finished the year with 6 goals and 42 assists and improved his plus/minus rating to a remarkable +28. With many years left in his career, it is without a doubt that Campbell's star will continue to rise, and one day, maybe, he will hold the Stanley Cup over his head.

Season	Team	GP	Goals	Assists	Points	+/-	Penalties
1999–2000	Buffalo	12	1	4	5	–2	4
2000–01	Buffalo	8	0	0	0	–2	2
2001–02	Buffalo	29	3	3	6	0	12
2002–03	Buffalo	65	2	17	19	–8	20
2003–04	Buffalo	53	3	8	11	–8	12
2005–06	Buffalo	79	12	32	44	–14	16
2006–07	Buffalo	82	6	42	48	28	35

Ryan Whitney

For a long time, most of the best players in the NHL were raised in the Canadian system of hockey, but as the game has grown in popularity, more and more young people from the United States are making their mark in the professional ranks. One of the better defensemen to make his way through the U.S. college hockey system is Ryan Whitney, who is currently scoring goals and stopping offensive rushes for the Pittsburgh Penguins.

Ryan Whitney began his path to the NHL when he enrolled at Thayer Academy in Braintree, Massachusetts, in 1998. He immediately impressed the coaches of the school's hockey team. Whitney was often paired up with Brooks Orpik, and the two defensemen formed the core of the Thayer defense. Just 16 years old at the time but towering close to six feet, four inches tall, Whitney was a solid positional defenseman but could also move his feet and the puck remarkably well.

His size and ability on the ice caught the U.S. National Hockey Team Development Program's attention, but Whitney resisted their offers, preferring to remain at Thayer Academy. However, the U.S. Program knew talent when they saw it and pursued Whitney until he accepted its offer and transferred to the Program for his senior year.

After a stellar senior year under the guidance of the National Program coaches, he accepted a full scholarship to Boston University.

Whitney had a solid season in 2001–02 playing for the Boston University Terriers, and when it came time for the 2002 NHL entry draft, many teams showed interest in the young defenseman. It was the Pittsburgh Penguins who got the lucky draw and selected Whitney fifth overall. Riding high on his draft selection, Whitney returned to Boston University to play another season and finish his studies. After completing university, he was shipped off to the Penguins' AHL affiliate, the Wilkes-Barre/Scranton Penguins, where he played one full season in 2004–05, scoring 6 goals and 35 assists. The Pittsburgh Penguins were eager to call up Whitney in the 2005–06 season to see if he could perform under the intense pressure of the NHL, but they were loaded with defensemen and would not sit out a veteran in favor of a rookie. When defenseman Dick Tarnstrom went out fairly early in the season with an injury, Whitney got his chance with the Penguins.

Assistant coach Michel Therrien had coached Whitney during his first year with the farm team and knew that the big defenseman would be an asset to the Penguins squad. Whitney played in

69 games that season and scored 6 goals and 32 assists but ended with a disappointing plus/minus rating of –7.

But mediocrity was never good enough for Whitney, and during the off-season, he worked heavily on conditioning his body and practicing his positional play. All the training and preparation paid off for Whitney and the Penguins as the young team went from missing the playoffs in 2005–06 to finishing the 2006–07 season with 105 points, good enough for fifth place in the Eastern Conference. Whitney's maturity showed on the ice and on the scoreboard. He now had a better idea of when to jump in on an offensive rush or hold back on defense. His scorecard improved, with 14 goals, 45 assists and a plus/minus rating of +9. The Penguins were taken out in the first round of the 2007 playoffs by the Ottawa Senators, but there is no doubt that this young team, led by forward and newly appointed captain Sidney Crosby and other young guys such as Ryan Whitney on defense, will be taking their team to new heights in seasons to come.

Season	Team	GP	Goals	Assists	Points	+/-	Penalties
2005–06	Pittsburgh	69	6	32	38	–7	85
2006–07	Pittsburgh	81	14	45	59	9	77

Notes on Sources

Basu, Arpon. *Hockey's Hottest Players.* Montréal: OverTime Books, 2005.

Diamond, Dan, ed. *Total NHL*. Toronto: Dan Diamond and Associates, 2003.

The Internet Hockey Database. http://www.hockeydb.com.

Johnson, George, et al. *Calgary Flames: The Fire Inside.* Toronto: CanWest Books, 2006.

Leonetti, Mike. *Canadiens Legends: Montreal's Hockey Heroes*. Vancouver: Raincoast Books, 2003.

———. *Maple Leaf Legends.* Vancouver: Raincoast Books, 2002.

Podnieks, Andrew, et al. *Kings of the Ice: A History of World Hockey.* Richmond Hill: NDE Publishing, 2002.

Rudd, Jeff. *Hockey's Young Superstars: The 25 Hottest Players on Ice*. Vancouver: Raincoast Books, 2003.

J. Alexander Poulton

J. Alexander Poulton is a writer and photographer and has been a genuine enthusiast of Canada's national pastime ever since seeing his first hockey game. His favorite memory is meeting the legendary gentleman hockey player Jean Béliveau, who in 1988 towered over the young awe-struck author.

Poulton earned his B.A. in English Literature from McGill University and his graduate diploma in Journalism from Concordia University. He has five other books to his credit: *Canadian Hockey Record Breakers, Greatest Moments in Canadian Hockey, Greatest Games of the Stanley Cup, The Montréal Canadiens* and *Greatest Goalies of the NHL*.